# PAM AND AL

# TOUR ROUND THE COAST OF BRITAIN

# IN OUR FIAT AUTOCRUISE JAZZ

In Stages from Monday 8th May 2017

until Tuesday 8th October 2019

63 Days, covering approximately 4674 miles.

Spanning times of great sadness and times of great worry but altogether a special and highly enjoyable experience and journey of discovery.

2020 First Edition

Printed by
Leiston Press
Unit 1 – 1b Masterlord Industrial Estate
Leiston
Suffolk
IP16 4JD
01728 8003003
www.leistonpress.com

ISBN: 978-1-911311-78-2

© Pam Hargreaves

All rights reserved. No part of this book may be reproduced, stored in a retrieval system, or transmitted in any form or by any means electronic, mechanical, photocopying, recording or otherwise, without the prior permission of the author

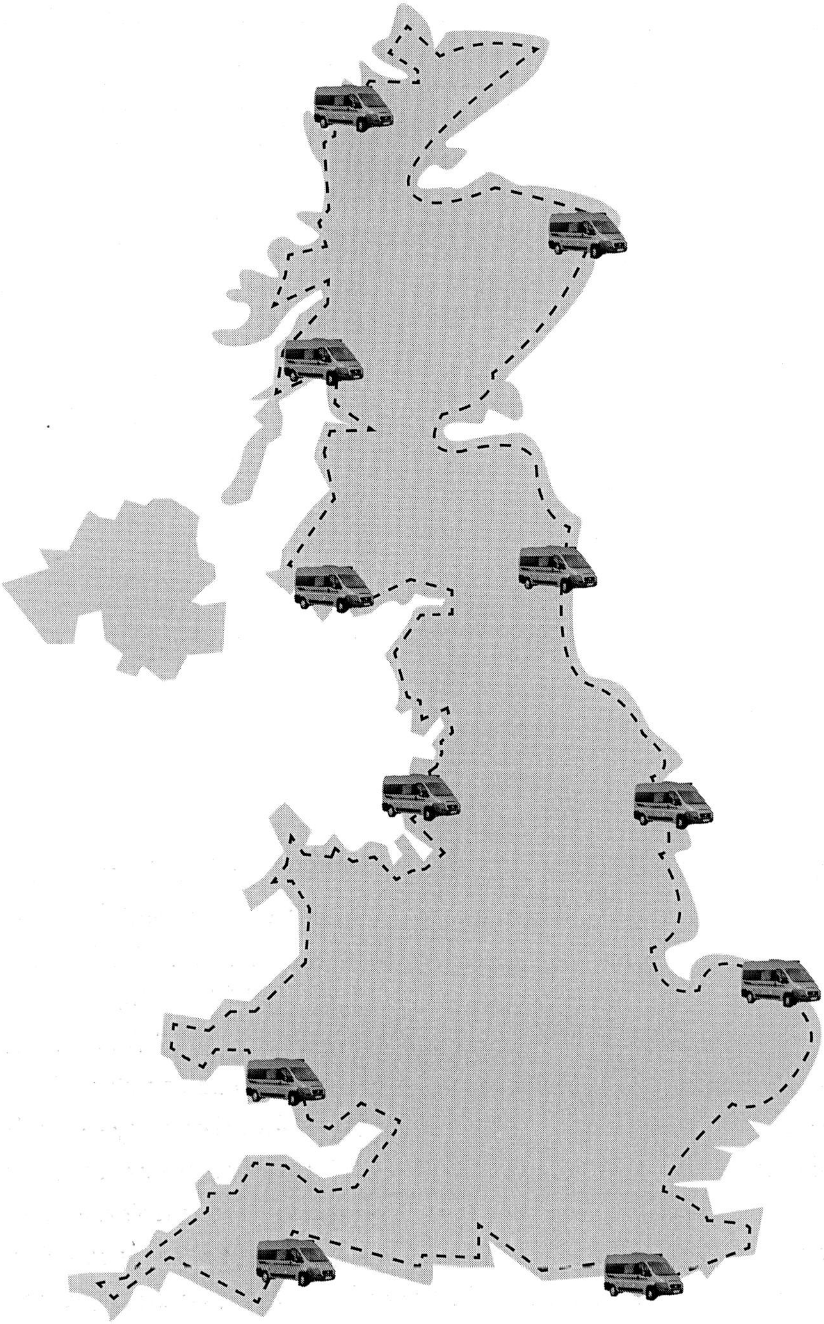

We have always enjoyed having an objective to our holidays having started by walking Wainwright's Coast to Coast for our honeymoon. Several walking holidays later, Alan's knee prevented him from walking long distances and so the idea of exploring the coast of Britain in our friendly motorhome emerged. Hearing that there were about 7,723 miles of coastline round Britain, we were aware that we couldn't go to every cove and corner but we determined to do our best, conscious of the limitations of a fairly cumbersome vehicle. With such an exciting project in mind we had no difficulty in deciding where to start, living just twenty miles from Lowestoft, the most easterly settlement and the most easterly point of the UK.

## MONDAY 8TH MAY 2017
## EAST ANGLIA

We set off for Lowestoft to do the first section of our journey as a day trip. Not being in too much of a hurry, we did some banking and shopping in Lowestoft town before heading for **Ness Point,** where we parked at the Maritime Museum (which we have yet to visit) and walked, in a bitterly cold wind, to the Ness. Working out that we could have parked there and wanting to be as authentic as possible, we retrieved the motorhome and found our way through the network of Birds Eye units, to drive to the **most easterly point**. This mass of industrial units, just behind the point, is built on the site of Lowestoft's original fishing village, known as the Grit, which was once home to 2,500 people, schools, churches, shops and 13 pubs. All of these are now gone, following the demise of the herring industry.  Lowestoft was, also, once famous for the production of porcelain, but this has also ceased.  We took pictures of ourselves, at the point, and of the fascinating plaques which show distances to such places as Lizard Point, Ardnamurchan Point and Dunnet Head.  We were off to visit them all.

After lunch in the van, we drove south past the Lowestoft beaches to view the pier and, on very familiar roads, we drove through Wrentham to the ever delightful Southwold.  I first spent a few, very hot, days at Southwold with Nicola, my daughter (also called Nic), in the 80's, and looking out from our B&B window thought it an inspiring and special place.  Alan and I are very fond of Southwold and its wonderfully eccentric pier, where we have our own plaque and where many of our family joined me for a 70$^{th}$ Birthday lunch, in February 2019.  We took further photos of the pier, and then, of the 102 foot tall lighthouse where I once suffered horrific vertigo.  Southwold has many greens, which arise from land left vacant after a disastrous fire in 1659.  We stopped on the harbour road, with a view of Walberswick, on other side of the river Blyth, to buy fresh halibut and headed home for our first RTC (Round The Coast) fish supper.    **26 miles**



### SATURDAY 20$^{TH}$ MAY 2017

Although Dunwich is on the coast, in fact much of it is now under the sea, we didn't visit this once medieval city of 4,000, on this occasion as it is not on a through route.  So, we started out from home at 10am and drove through very familiar Thorpeness, which was originally a fishing village called Thorpe but was renamed by the wealthy Scottish barrister Glencairn Stuart Ogilvie after he created 'an adult playground' inspired by the book written by his friend J. M. Barrie. Many features of 'Neverland' are to be found, most notably the Mere, a boating lake inspired by Peter Pan. The House in the Clouds, which was originally a water tower built in 1923, stands oddly above the village. We continued on through Aldeburgh and Snape. These are also very familiar towns for us. On the sea front of Aldeburgh, by the fishing huts, sits the Moot Hall, built in 1520 a Grade 1 listed timber framed building, used for council meetings for over 400 years, now a museum. On the beach, at Aldeburgh, is Maggi Hambling's famous, four metres high, sculpture called The Scallop, which stands as a tribute to Benjamin Britten who was born in Lowestoft but lived and worked in Aldeburgh for most of his life. In 2015, we saw some of Britten's 'Peter Grimes' performed on Aldeburgh beach.

We continued on to the Snape Maltings where we have seen several performances and where we went to see Father Christmas arrive on a Wherry, the last time that Derek, Alan's dear son, came to visit with his wife Sarah and children Lucy and Tom. This was just a few weeks before Derek died. So difficult for Alan to visit now, especially at Christmas. Continuing on, we stopped for coffee in a woody lay-by near Tunstall, then continued on through Woodbridge and on to Felixstowe. Having visited Felixstowe Ferry before, initially on our first outing together in 1995, we turned right towards the port and beach. Great decision.

We discovered Languard Fort which is English Heritage and therefore free to us members. Very interesting and well worth further visits. It is a polygonal fort started in the 18th Century, updated in Victorian times and later, in 1951, part of it became a Cold War control room. The Fort defends the approach to Harwich Harbour and an earlier fort there was the site of the **last opposed**

**seaborne invasion of England** when the Royal Marines repulsed a Dutch attack in 1667. Today it is by Felixsowe container port which is the **UK's busiest container port**, dealing with 48% of Britain's containerised trade. In 2017, it was ranked as 43rd busiest container port in the world and 8th in Europe. Fascinating to watch but not surprising that the A14 is so busy.

We had egg sandwiches in the motorhome and then took the short but exciting ferry to Harwich. By taking time to visit Harwich then we hoped to have more time to visit the north coast of Essex the next day. We boarded the small ferry from the beach and found Harwich to be unexpectedly interesting. We walked to see Ha'penny pier which is one of the **UK's only surviving wooden, working piers**. The name refers to the 1/2d (half an old penny) toll charged to passengers on the paddle steamer. We also walked to the Treadwheel Crane which is a wooden, human powered hoisting and lowering device which was primarily used during the Roman period and the Middle Ages in the building of castles and cathedrals.

We saw both the Low and High Lighthouses and the Napoleonic Redoubt. Back at the pier we saw the Floating Lighthouse which was used by Pirate radio stations in the 1960's. Apparently, there is a group trying to reconstruct the Mayflower but we were unable to see this.

We had a choppy return to Felixstowe and drove along the Stour estuary and into Essex, which some say has the longest coastline in Britain, however this is disputed by Cornwall, see later. We passed **Manningtree which is England's smallest town** and where the 'Witchfinder General' was born and buried. We saw the two Mistley Towers which are the only surviving part of a church designed by Robert Adam in the Eighteenth Century. We had some difficulty finding our CL site at Great Oakley but it was good when we got there although our Thai curries hadn't thawed and we had to wait. Time to write the journal and have a glass of wine.

## SUNDAY 21ST MAY, 2017

We left the 'field' at 9.15 am and took a ziggy zaggy route to Holland on Sea which had wonderful sandy beaches. Then to Clacton which was also sandy but also had lots of amusements and nowhere to park and take photos. We went back up the estuary to Colchester and found a carpark with no barriers and only £1 for the whole day's parking. Just the thing to cheer up Alan. So near but not visited properly before, we found Colchester impressive. The Priory ruins were beautiful as was Colchester Castle. The **Norman Keep is Europe's largest** and well preserved. Colchester (Camulodunon) is **Britain's oldest recorded town** and the **first Roman capital in England**. It was sacked by Boudicca in AD61 and there are said to be scorch marks from her carriage still to be seen on the castle walls. We had a pleasant walk round the well kept gardens before returning to the motorhome. There was some confusion getting out of Colchester on a sunny Sunday lunch time and there was much congestion, probably because the A14 was closed.

We headed towards Maldon and stopped at Promonade Park by the Blackwater Estuary. Interesting to be there, as I was in the process of reading The Essex Serpent by Sarah Perry, a story set on the Blackwater Estuary. We could see the town of Maldon, famous for its sea salt and for a battle in 991CE. We had a healthy salad and rice lunch in the van and a short walk before continuing our journey to Burnham on Crouch. We parked near a play park and had a short sleep before having a fabulous walk along the Crouch towards town. There were stunning colours but low tide so not much sailing. We had tea in delightful tea rooms with a very pretty garden dappled with hot sun. Once back in the motorhome we resumed onward journey with a view to finishing the coast of Essex.  Down to Shoeburyness where there was no place to park even briefly for a photo. It looked sandy, popular and expensive. Lovely coast.

We drove through Southend which was vibrant even at 6pm, with masses of amusements and gardens. The pier looked splendid. It extends 1.34 miles into the Thames estuary and is the **longest pier in the world.** We walked along it a few years previously on a visit to Peter and Bee, Alan's cousin and his wife, together with Alan's other cousins Christopher and Alison. Bee and Peter were not at home, on this occasion,so we couldn't visit. We enjoyed the admirable views from Westcliff before continuing on through Leigh on Sea, with its many cockle and winkle huts, before progressing along the estuary and fearing queues on M25, we bought some sandwiches at a petrol station to 'keep us going' and cut through to the A12, ensuring we had correct mileage before leaving the coast. Home at 9pm, but a most enjoyable day.

199 miles over last two days, **total = 225 miles** so far.

## TUESDAY 13TH JUNE, 2017

### SOUTH

After a break of about a month we set off again towards Kent, my county of birth. We left home at 10.30am following final liaisons with Chris King concerning the relaying of our patio. We then *had to* stop at Waitrose to buy wine at 25% off and had coffee in the car park there. We drove down the A12, A130 and A13 to reach the point where we had finished previously. We checked the mileage and continued on to the Dartford crossing, over the Queen Elizabeth 2nd Bridge , which was opened in 1991 and is now **the busiest estuarial crossing in the UK**. We then drove along the north coast of Kent past Gravesend to Chatham Dockyard. Beginning in Gravesend and continuing round the coast to Hastings in East Sussex, is the Saxon Shore Way, which links shore forts built by the Romans and seen off by the Saxons. Our visit to Chatham Dockyard was very interesting and in great heat, always a pleasure. This was a Royal Navy Dockyard located on the river Medway in the mid 16th century and is now a museum. We looked at several historic vessels and had a conducted tour of the fascinating submarine Ocelet, accompanied by a large number of French school children, also enjoying a visit. From parts of the site we could see the Elizabethan Upnor Castle, which was built in 1559, to protect warships in Chatham dockyard. We then had a short journey to our certified camp site at Upchurch. It was a large field by an orchard with sheep in surrounding fields. Very rural and peaceful.

34 miles so **total = 259** .

## WEDNESDAY 14TH JUNE, 2017

Up at 6am !! Sunny, cuckoos singing and already very hot. Left site at 8.30ish and drove through Sittingbourne, Faversham and Whitstable, where I went for a zoology field trip in 1966. We drank our coffee on the grass above the beach at Herne Bay, a wonderful vista, and drove through very narrow lanes to get to Reculver Towers, which we couldn't visit as there was a barrier over the car park. Very annoying, and one of the downsides of travelling in a motorhome. These 12th century towers are all that remains of an atmospheric seaside church, enclosing traces of a Saxon monastery. I snatched a photo and we then got lost in the narrow lanes before driving on to Margate with great views of Foreness Point.

We continued on through Broadstairs and Ramsgate with stunning views of sun drenched Pegwell Bay and on to Richborough Roman Fort. It was still very hot and we didn't delay in Broadstairs, Margate or Ramsgate as we had been there with Bee and Peter two years earlier. A bit of a shame as there would have been things to see particularly Ramsgate harbour, which is **the only Royal Harbour in the UK** because of its proximity to Europe. It was the chief embarkation point during the Napoleonic wars and for the Dunkirk evacuation. Perhaps, we could even have visited the Tate Modern, if Alan had allowed.

However, Richborough Castle was special It contains the ruins of a Roman Saxon Shore Fort , collectively known as Richborough Roman Fort. Now owned by English Heritage meant we did not to have to pay. A wonderful site especially when drenched in sun. This site witnessed both the **beginning and almost the end of Roman rule in Britain**. It is two miles inland now but in AD 43 it overlooked a sheltered channel where the invading **Roman**

**forces first came ashore.** It was from here that the **first Roman road** was built, Watling Street, and it ran from here to Chester. We looked but couldn't see evidence of it. We continued to Deal but didn't visit the castle again, it had been very cold and wet two years previously.

We didn't visit Walmer Castle again either, not tempted to see **Wellington's boots** again, although I might have enjoyed the gardens a second time. Alan drove to NT White Cliffs, where we walked a short way to get a stunning view of the cliffs and magnificent blue sea. It was on this coast that Caesar first attempted to invade but he was deterred by the weather. It was also here on Christmas Eve 1914, that the **first ever air raid of Britain** occurred. We had great views of Dover Port and Castle, of which we had a conducted tour two years ago. The castle, the **biggest in Britain**, has a 2000 year history and is renowned as **'the Key to England'**.

It was lovely to watch the ferries entering and leaving the port. It was so hot that Alan had to buy an expensive but more protective NT hat. I then continued driving on coast roads through Dover and Folkstone to Hythe but then confusing instructions caused consternation and we didn't arrive at site until 6pm. Site manager surprised that we were so late! Shame, as it had been a brilliant and informative day.

93 miles, so **total = 352**

# THURSDAY 15ᵀᴴ JUNE, 2017

Set off at 9.30am, with Alan driving down the coast via Dymchurch and New Romney to remote Dungeness. We have memories of walking there a few years before, having great difficulty walking over the pebbles and being relieved to get to the platform to pick up the Romney, Hythe and Dymchurch train (**smallest passenger railway in the world** )back to the motorhome, which we had hired in order to try out motorhoming!

Dungeness is **Britain's only desert** and is **one of Europe's largest expanses of shingle**. It is said to be the most 'Europhile part of Britain' because it is growing towards France at about a yard a year! It has an old and a new lighthouse and a large Nuclear Power Station. The area was rich in beautiful blue Purple Bugloss, when we visited. We had an unfortunately short visit to the RSPB Nature Reserve, visiting only one hide and seeing black headed gulls, coots and oyster catchers.

We returned to continue our trip through Lydd and Camber, where I often visited for family days out when I was a child. It was from Lydd that I flew for the first time, in 1966, when my father, ex RAF and very keen on planes, excitedly arranged for us, and the car, to go on holiday to France. Coincidently, it was also from here that Alan had his first flight abroad, when he went with his parents to Paris. The airport is privately owned and still caters for a range of aircraft.

I managed to get a distant photo of Camber Castle, which is one of Henry V111's artillery forts and built to guard the port of Rye. Rye was busy with no obvious sort stay parking. It looked very attractive and I managed to get a photo of the Ypres tower, also known as Rye Castle, which is two miles inland but used to be on the coast. Rye, which was formerly a subsidiary of New Romney, is one of the Cinque Ports, the others are Hastings, Hythe, Dover and Sandwich.

We continued on through Hastings, which was much smarter than we recalled, and then got stuck in traffic at Bexhill on Sea. We got to Pevensey but had trouble parking as the car park had a height barrier. We managed to park in a small lane but Alan was worried that the motorhome might get scratched if we left it unattended. I had a quick look at the castle, which looked wonderful, and I managed a couple of quick photos before getting us out of the tight lane. Pevensey Castle was a massive Roman Fortress, strong medieval castle and emergency Second World War stronghold. It was **the largest of the Roman 'Saxon Shore' fortresses** and it was here, in 1066, that **William the Conqueror landed** to begin his invasion of England, building a fortress within the Roman defences. We bought sandwiches on the outskirts of Eastbourne and drove to Beachy Head to eat them. Fantastic location but as we arrived, and after all the hot weather, the clouds came down making visibility very limited.

I was surprised/impressed/concerned by the number of posters for Samaritans and by a parked car with 'Beachy Head Chaplaincy' on the side. We drove leisurely through the stunning Downs to Birling Gap, where we had fabulous views of the Seven Sisters, England's iconic chalk cliffs of the south coast. There are now eight peaks and each has its own name. It was very windy and the sea was dramatic, a stunning and popular spot. We then continued on the coast road through Newhaven, Peacehaven and other high cliff towns, such as Rottingdean to get to Brighton, which was horribly busy, at rush hour. We noted our mileage and headed up to Senlac site where we would spend some time with Bee and Peter.

Today 97 miles **Total = 445 miles.**

## SATURDAY 17TH JUNE, 2017

We had two pleasant 'holiday' nights at Senlac site. On the 16th June we visited Battle and Battle Castle, where we had an excellent audio tour of the castle and the site of the Battle of Hastings. It was very well presented. In the evening Bee and Peter arrived and we had a delicious meal with them at a pub that they had enjoyed previously. In the morning we stayed to have coffee with them before returning to the coast, avoiding Brighton (Britain's answer to Hollywood), as we have visited before. We continued through other coastal places Hove, Worthing, Littlehampton and Middleton on Sea, where Nicola used to live close to the sea. Having visited these places many times over the years, we went straight to Flansham to stay with Nic and her husband Graham, where they now live. Just 28 miles **Total = 473**

## MONDAY 19TH JUNE, 2017

Two lovely days with Nic and Graham including a visit to Worthing to see Nic do 'Race for Life'. It was a beautiful sunny day and Alan, Graham and I had a delightful walk along the pier eating ice cream while Nicola ran! The area around Worthing contains **Britain's greatest concentration of Stone Age flint mines**, which are **some of the earliest mines in Europe**. We also knew the next stretch of coast well so drove steadily along the A27 past Chichester and Portsmouth until we got to Eastleigh where we took note of the mileage. Chichester is a delightful walled, cathedral city and it has been a settlement since Roman times. Nearby are the very well preserve remains of Fishbourne Roman Palace which is the **largest Roman building discovered in Britain** and has an unusually early date of 75 AD.  The mosaics are fantastic.  Portsmouth is also an interesting city with its Historic Dockyard home to many historic vessels including the Victory and the Tudor Mary Rose. However, Portsmouth is strictly an island and on our tour we were only covering the mainland.

A little later, at Eastleigh, we took note of the mileage and headed north to London, where we were to stay with Norma and Philip, my older sister and her husband, before returning home.

We had now covered the coasts of Suffolk, Essex, Kent and Sussex and were so excited about picking up in Hampshire later in the year.

47 miles.  **Total = 520**

Change of plan! In order to accommodate a holiday on the Isles of Scilly, we jumped to Cornwall in September 2017. However, we decided to continue the journal chronologically. To pick up where we left off in Hampshire, we had to wait until March 2018, when we, particularly Alan, were rather different people. For details of that stretch see later.

## WEDNESDAY 13TH SEPTEMBER, 2017

## SOUTH WEST

So, we continued our Round Britain Tour in our Motorhome after a long summer break. Jumping to Cornwall in order to facilitate a holiday on the Isles of Scilly added an extra excitement. There is some debate as to whether Cornwall or Essex has the longer coastline in Britain, however Ordnance Survey state that **Cornwall has the longest coastline**, although, as said, Essex remains unsure about this. Whatever, it was our intention to see as much of the Cornish coast that our motorhome would allow. We stayed with Ruth and Pete, Alan's sister and her husband, the night before getting to Cornwall and started our mileage count at Plymouth, intending to fill in the Hampshire to Cornwall mileage later.

Crossing the Tamar Toll Bridge was amazingly exciting, the sun was shining and we had a pleasant journey to our motorhome site just outside Looe. A grass standing, so we hoped there would be no rain. Helpful staff directed us to where we could get a bus into Looe where we had a delightful walk round this very pretty, but touristy, fishing town. It has a lovely beach and coast. I bought a long searched for leather rucksack and then we bought two pasties from that year's winning pasty makers. There were an amazing number of different varieties from which to choose but we managed. Unusually, we invested in a taxi back to the site and had a delicious supper of pasties, home grown courgettes and left over beans – a feast. Happy plans for the next day, so much to see in this county so far from home.

Eighteen miles **Total = 552**

## THURSDAY 14TH SEPTEMBER, 2017

A fairly early start at 9.15 am, meant we arrived early at Polperro. We wanted to see it but not delay, and parking was £9 for the day, we didn't stay or see this fishing village said to be one of the most popular in Britain. Our next coastal stop was at Fowey where we parked in a car park above the town and walked down to sea level. We found this a very attractive town sitting on the Fowey estuary with St Catherine's Castle, built by Henry V111, standing at the edge of the harbour. Fowey is where Daphne du Maurier lived and worked and 'Manderley' is based on a nearby village. On the opposite side of the estuary sits Polruan which appeared to have an extremely steep street which, from where we were, looked like a waterfall. With some difficulty Alan managed it back up to the car park and we drove round the coast south of St. Austell to Charlestown.

We eventually parked and walked down to this fascinating heritage town. It has square rigged ships in its traditional harbour and these ships and the surroundings are regularly used in period films, including Poldark. As we arrived several horse boxes were leaving and one of the vessels was being pulled back into position. It seems we just missed some filming. Great spot. Anxious about the narrow lanes, we took the main road to our next camp site just outside Portscutto. A quick cup of tea and then we went out again to St. Mawes. We drove through this smart town and visited the English Heritage Castle built by Henry V111. It is **one of the best preserved military fortresses,** built by Henry and beautifully positioned on the Roseland peninsular. We had a very interesting tour before driving back to the site for a pizza starter and 'Cooks' pork and mustard meal. Lovely.

70 miles **Total = 622**

## FRIDAY 15TH SEPTEMBER, 2017

Set off at 9.30am, in the rain, and headed for St. Just in Roseland, a fabulous, pretty and delightful place. Subtropical gardens stretch down to the water side 13th century church and there are stone inscriptions from the Bible on the track down and around the church yard. Inside was pretty and ordered with, probably, a hundred, beautifully worked kneelers portraying flowers, animals and a variety of scenes. We had an interesting talk to the verger. Unsurprisingly, this is **one of Cornwall's most visited churches**. Unfortunately, it wasn't until later that I realised that Nancy, my Scottish cousin David's wife, came from this village.

It had been quite good exercise walking down and back from the church, so we had coffee before driving on, in alternating sunshine and showers, towards King Harry's Ferry. As we crossed the River Fal it rained and it continued to rain solidly as we visited NT Trelissick House and gardens. Wonderful, diverse and abundant gardens with panoramic views down to the sea, but not at their best in the rain. We had lunch in the motorhome, stocked up at an Asda and found our next site near Falmouth. We then walked about a mile and a half, through a quite uninspiring housing estate, into Falmouth. The town centre didn't inspire us much but the harbour, which is the **world's third largest natural harbour**, was quite impressive albeit functional in appearance. We bought ready meal curries from a small Tesco and caught a very old bus back to the site. That was an unexpectedly interesting journey providing a scenic tour of the beaches and a humorous commentary from the driver.

29 miles  **Total = 651**


## SATURDAY 16<sup>TH</sup> AND SUNDAY 17<sup>TH</sup> SEPTEMBER, 2017

Two busy days with lots to see and experience. We left Falmouth in the rain and headed, in the rain, to Pendennis Castle, EH. We went round the castle in the rain and had a tour of the magazines in the rain. Another of Henry V111's castles built as protection against the French. It has Tudor guns, WW1 guardhouse and WW11 exhibition. The café served a very welcome thick carrot and sweet potato soup.

We drove via Helston, **Britain's southernmost town**, and on to find the next site, where we reserved our spot in a farm field before heading down to Lizard Point, the **southernmost point of mainland Britain**. This is a splendid headland with rugged rocks jutting into the sea. It is dominated by the fortress-like lighthouse, first established in 1612. We had a short, bracing walk before returning to the farm where we got stuck trying to get onto our selected place on the field. We received advice and help from others on the field and eventually from the farmer's wife and son in their Land Rover. However, it took the farmer and his brand new JCB 'all purpose farm vehicle' to pull us out of the mud.

After a short drive to get some mud off the tyres we parked on a semi-solid piece of field that we all thought safe. All in the rain. A very good meal was had at the Wheel Inn and a good night's sleep. There was no shower to be seen and the toilet was ramshackle, surprising for such a smart farm. However, when we tried to move the motorhome we found that we were stuck again and once more had to be towed to sound ground. We were eventually able to continue on our way round the magnificent Mount's Bay, not visiting Porthleven, **Britain's most southerly port**. As so often happens, it was difficult to find somewhere for a brief stop, just to look and take a photo, so we had to carry on. However, we hovered in Marazion for a while and took a photo of St. Michael's Mount, and drove slowly through Penzance and the very pretty villages of Newlyn, the **largest working fishing port in Britain**, and Mousehole. Mousehole is named for its small harbour and tight harbour mouth. It is a picturesque fishing village with notoriously narrow streets and alleyways and is not recommended for wider vehicles. We shouldn't have been there and hadn't intended to be there but suddenly there we were, with wing mirrors in and people pinned against the walls, looking over the wall at the beautiful harbour. There was no turning back, so we edged our way through and onto a wider, narrow road. Dylan Thomas had a friend living in Mousehole and, having visited, was said to be inspired to write 'Under Milk Wood'.

Our next stop was to see Minack Theatre, Cornwall's famous open air theatre opened in the 1930's. It is built into the sheer cliff overlooking the stunning Porthcurno Bay.  Everything was glistening in the sun, but I couldn't be encouraged to go down to see the seats or the stage.  I could see enough from the top of the cliff.  Nearby was the Porthcurno Telegraph Museum which is all about the history of international communications which were centred here from 1870 – 1970.  Cornish miners dug tunnels to house the entire telegraph operations during World War 11.  Such a shame that we were unable to visit the museum.  We drove south to Land's End, named Bolerium or 'Seat of Storms' by the Romans.  It is a very touristy place but quite fun to visit.

We proceeded to our next site overlooking Sennan Cove and airport. Sennan Cove is the **most westerly surf spot** in the country, has white sand and clear turquoise water.  I did some washing in the site machine and Alan did some motorhome maintenance.  We packed, cooked supper and got excited about our flight to the Scillies the next morning.

72 miles  **Total = 723**

## MONDAY 25TH SEPTEMBER, 2017

Back from a wonderful, relaxing and interesting week on the Isles of Scilly. The motorhome started with no problem and we commenced our journey up the north coast of Cornwall.  Our first stop was to see the Lavant mine and Beam Engine – NT.  It sits in a splendid setting on the edge of a cliff and was very interesting.  The mine stretched a mile out to sea at a depth of 2,000feet.  The unique steam-powered Cornish beam engine is the **only one in the world still in steam** on its original site and, to Alan's enormous joy it was working when we visited. We drove on to St Ives, unfortunately missing Zennor which has a carved mermaid on one of the church's bench ends.

We found our good big site at St.Ives and walked to the harbour for lunch looking at the sea. Lovely sunshine. Later, we visited the Barbara Hepworth museum where we spent a considerable amount of time and took several photos. We happily wandered through this pretty, clean, artist's town, eating ice cream, before shopping in the Spar and returning to the site for M&S tinned Thai Chicken curry – ok.

18 miles **Total = 741**


## TUESDAY 26TH SEPTEMBER, 2017

Left St. Ives at 9.30ish (just for a change) and eventually found the coast road to Hayle, but we didn't go to RSPB Hayle as we were limited on time. So, we went on to have coffee by the harbour at Portreath. There is a very narrow entrance to the harbour here and it is hard to believe that a large ship could navigate such a tight space, however it was once a **key port for the export of the area's copper**. It now has a lovely sandy beach. We returned to Redruth which was once one of Cornwall's wealthiest towns because of the area's profitable mineral mining, and we had to take the A30 for a short distance before returning to as near to the coast as seemed sensible in our vehicle.

We continued on past Perranporth, which is home to St. Piran's Cross, the only three holed cross in Cornwall. This site is, probably, **the oldest place of worship in Britain**. Further on is the vast town of Newquay, which appears to have sea on all sides. It is the

**UK's surf capital** and Cornwall's best known tourist town. We passed through and continued on the 'up and down' coast road which felt similar to the South West Coast Walk, some of which I walked in 1994. At Mawgan Porth there was a beautiful sandy beach with several surfers hurrying towards it. Perhaps the tide was just turning or the word had gone out about the conditions, but they were certainly eager. We bought beans in the little shop and had cheese sandwiches in the free carpark.

Having visited Padstow a few year's previously and fearing the congestion, it was with some regret that we didn't visit again but, instead, continued on round the edge of the town, then through Wadebridge and past St. Minver, where John Betjeman is buried. Then to the delightful Tintagel. I had a magical stay here with Nicola, possibly 35 years ago, when we stayed in a tiny Youth Hostel on the edge of the cliffs. From it one could see no manmade objects. I also walked through here with Wellingborough Ramblers on the aforementioned walk in 1994. This time, we parked in a pub carpark where we could have camped for the night.

We went to view the castle, Alan from a closer point than I could manage. Very vertiginous! It is a spectacular and magical place and birth place of King Arthur? There is evidence of Dark Age connections between Spain and Cornwall and the discovery of the 'Arthnou' stone suggests this was a **royal place for Dark Age rulers of Cornwall.** We found our campsite in a stunning position on a high cliff overlooking the sea. Great weather.

93 miles **Total = 816**

## WEDNESDAY 27TH SEPTEMBER, 2017

We left Tintagel site, having filled and emptied as necessary, in readiness for a Certificated site, about which Alan was quite anxious. It was cloudy, with rain and wind forecast, actually, it was already very windy. We drove through Boscastle, another Youth Hostelling venue for Nicola and me. It was as pretty as always. We then drove north to Bude, then back to Widemouth Bay where we had coffee overlooking the wide bay. It was raining but there was a stream of surfers heading for the sea, they appeared to be school children having a lesson. We drove out of Cornwall and in to Devon in the rain and on to Hartland Quay.

I am so pleased that we didn't miss this fascinating and atmospheric place. It was a tricky drive down towards the grim, sharp rocks and vicious seas. The quay here was destroyed in 1800's and the story is told in the interesting museum. There is also a great pub, The Wreckers Retreat, where we had lunch. Alan had fish and chips and I had a baked potato with prawns, lovely. We drove back up the peninsular and passed the road down to Clovelly as that private village is, allegedly, steep, expensive and touristy. As Alan was still anxious, we drove to our next site which was isolated but in a good, rural position.

We went to pay at the farm house and were met by an elderly lady who wanted to chat and give us tea, which, on this occasion, we declined. We thought we might visit Barnstaple in the rain, but only got as far as Asda, before returning to our hardstanding.

78 miles **Total = 894.**

## THURSDAY 28TH SEPTEMBER, 2017

I woke at 6.50am with an urgent need for the toilet so walked to the one allocated at the side of the farm house, quite a long way. It was barely light but there was a beautiful sunrise. The alpacas in the field next to us looked up and their eyes followed me but it was clearly too early for them to stand. We consequently had an early start at 8.50am and got caught in the Barnstaple business traffic. We could have visited Braunton Beaches where preparations for the Normandy Landings were made, but, instead, continued on to Woolacombe.

It was delightfully sunny which gave the wonderful, wide, sandy beach a 'picture postcard' appearance. I came here for a family holiday when I was quite young and recalled that it was sunny then too. We had coffee in Ilfracombe near some rocks and drove through the 'amusements' area and past a pretty harbour. Again, as there were no suitable roads we climbed on to Exmoor and followed the A39 to Linton. Exmoor was beautiful but the roads became increasingly narrow and winding. We had a short walk in Lynton but I didn't fancy going on the Lynton and Lynmouth Cliff Railway, spoil sport, as Alan would have loved it.

As it had been tricky getting in, we asked for advice on the best road out. Not sure that we got good advice. We had a precarious drive down into Lynmouth and on a stretch of road barely wide enough for one vehicle, we met a large beer delivery lorry and he was not going to back up! I needed to reverse quite a way and was quite shaken, but my anxiety increased as we drove out of Lynmouth on a cliff edge, still the A39. It was a real white knuckle drive for me and I used the central white line as the centre of my steering. Fortunately, nothing came in the opposite direction. Some people might call that a road with a splendid view, Alan thought it was, but not me. We were soon able to stop and recover at a view point / picnic spot where we had our lunchtime sandwiches. Phew! Into Somerset and onto Porlock, on a much more sensible road, where we had a pleasant walk out onto the marshes.

Porlock is a pretty coastal village much favoured by the Romantic poets such as Coleridge, Shelley and Wordsworth. In 2010, it had the **most elderly population in Britain**, with 40% being over pensionable age. Westleton must be close on its heels for that record! We got to our site at Minehead early at 2.30pm and could have gone to visit Minehead or Dunster Castle, which is an elegant former motte and bailey castle now a country house owned by the National Trust. Or, we could have visited the West Somerset Railway but I was exhausted and thinking of our long Journey home.

71 miles  **Total = 965**


## FRIDAY 29TH SEPTEMBER, 2017

After a very rainy and windy night we set off at 9.30ish, expecting a wet journey home, however, it was sunny when we left and dry most of the day. We were not sure which route to take but wanted to avoid the M25. It took ages to get to and around Bridgwater and we didn't see much of the coast or Severn Estuary. The best road then was the M5, as we had both visited Weston- Super-Mare before. We didn't visit Bristol either, as we were there two years ago and Alan knows it well from his years as a dental student. We did miss some great opportunities for bird watching, eg. at

Brean Down, and there were potential National Trust places to go to as well, but we had been away for over two weeks and home was calling. We took note of the mileage at the M5/M4 junction, ready to pick up our coastal mileage record when we continued into Wales.

64 miles   **Total = 1029**

We had coffee when we reached the M4 and thought that a good place to have a break would be Kettering, so we rang Derek, and arranged to see him, Sarah, Lucy and Tom, together with their new puppy later, in the day. We had lunch on the A45 near Towcester and progressed on to Kettering where we met the delightful Luna. Clearly the whole family was completely in love with this puppy "that they were never going to have".

We managed to get home for 8pm and went for dinner at the pub, where we later met up with friends, Fiona and Clive. All great!

Over 1000 miles, to date, and looking forward to getting going again, probably in the New Year.

## SUNDAY 25TH MARCH, 2018

So much sadness since our last trip and so difficult to get moving. The sudden death of Derek had devastated Alan and his family. Bravely, Alan felt he was able to go to his nephew Luke's Wedding in Burford, so we decided that as we were there we might as well continue down to fill in the missing gap in our journey round the coast. The wedding was a mixed happy and sad event and the next day we had coffee with Carol and Richard, Alan's daughter and her husband, then set off to have lunch in the motorhome at Eastleigh with Nicola and Graham. Nicola had just done a run in the area and was looking well.

We took note of our mileage at the M3/M27 junction and continued round Southampton and on our way. Southampton is **Britain's oldest continuously active port**, but we didn't get to see much of it owing to the massive oil refineries. We drove down the side of Southampton Water to Calshot Castle, which was, unfortunately, closed. It is an English Heritage Tudor artillery fort built to defend the approaches to Southampton. Having seen and visited much of the Hampshire coast previously, we drove on and stopped in Lymington, to buy a camera card, one thing I had completely forgotten to buy. We then went on through New Milton, where Alan used to have family, and through the very pretty New Forest, with ponies roaming around, and on to our camp site at Bransgore. It was a lovely site and not very busy. We sat with the door open in the sun, listened to birdsong and began to relax and feel the joy of being away and free to explore. However, Alan was quite contemplative and anxious, having been found to have a major heart problem himself, and he was sad at not being able to drive. However, his navigating skills were well up to speed.

51 miles  **Total = 1080 miles**

## MONDAY 26TH MARCH, 2018

A very pleasant, interesting and relaxing day, so good for us. We left the New Forest site at 10am and stopped for coffee on the sea front at Southbourne. It was sunny and we overlooked the sea and beach where Alan used to take Carol and Derek, when they were little. We drove on through Bournemouth with some lovely views of Poole Bay. Then on through Poole with views of the harbour, **the second largest natural harbour in the world**. We went round the harbour and a long way out to RSPB Arne, where we had lunch and a lovely walk taking another great view of Poole Harbour. We didn't see many birds but there were some elegant Roe Deer with their young. It was delightfully sunny as we drove to Corfe Castle, with fabulous views of the castle enroute. We found our site, had tea and walked back to see the castle more closely. The castle, its buildings and most of the village are built in the local Purbeck stone. The building began in 1086 and it later became one of Britain's greatest strongholds until it was destroyed, by the Parliamentarians, in 1646. We had a pleasant walk through the town and took a photo of The Greyhound, said to be **the most photographed pub in Britain,** possibly because of its excellent views of the castle. Before supper, we went on to Studland for a short, breezy and chilly walk. From there we could look across to Sandbanks which has the **fourth most expensive land on the planet.** Studland beach is two and a half miles long. We returned via Swanage to our site for our supper of Cook's Beef Casserole. We were then on the **Jurassic Coast which is 95 miles long** and is **Britain's only natural World Heritage Site**. The Jurassic Coast starts at Old Harry Rocks, from where, 2000 years ago, the mainland connected to the Isle of Wight.

61 miles    **Total = 1141**

## TUESDAY 27ᵀᴴ MARCH, 2018

Early rise at 7am after a restless night. Raining! Slow to do jobs but left at 10am for Lulworth Cove. We found the Visitor centre to be very interesting and we watched an informative film about the area. At Lulworth there are five layers of rock, which are millions of years old. The oldest and strongest rock is Portland stone. The Cove was formed about 10,000 years ago, the combined forces of a river and the sea hollowed out the soft clays to reveal the hard chalk behind. It is a Site of Special Scientific Interest, an Area of Outstanding Natural Beauty and is part of the World Heritage coastline.

The weather improved slightly as we drove to Durdle Door and walked down to the viewing platform. The rock here is mainly limestone. We then drove on to Weymouth to find our site and have lunch in the motorhome. We could have, but didn't, continue on to the Abbotsbury Swannery, which was established by Benedictine Monks who built a monastery at Abbotsbury during the 1040's. The monks farmed the swans to produce food for their lavish banquets. We didn't go to Abbotsbury Subtropical gardens either, mainly because of the damp weather. Instead, we went into Weymouth, where we initially had difficulty parking, but found a place and walked to Nothe Fort, had views of the lovely beaches and enjoyed the pretty gardens overlooking the sea.

Nothe Fort was built by the Victorians to protect Weymouth harbour, 'D' shaped, it is one of the **best preserved forts of its kind**. We returned to the motorhome and drove off, not knowing that there would be a parking charge when we got home. (Possibly, Alan keyed in the wrong registration number but it led to many discussions with Parking Eye! We did, eventually, get the charge reduced to £20 administration fee). However, our site was set in lovely fields and over looked Chesil Beach, which sparkled in the silvery, damp sunlight.

43 miles   **Total = 1184**

## WEDNESDAY 28TH MARCH, 2018

This would have been my mother's 100th Birthday.

It was late up for me but I was feeling much better. There was serious rain as we went to the shower block and found rooms with shower, sink and toilet all in together, very helpful. We filled and emptied the motorhome and set off to Abbotsbury village where we saw the Abbey remains and the Tythe Barn, which is the **longest in Britain,** (84m ) and thatched with local reed. We continued on along this beautiful coast in the rain but, despite this, the sea was a wonderfully varied range of colours.

We didn't go to Golden Gap, which is the highest point on England's south coast, but went on to Charmouth, reknowned for the fossils found on its beach. In the Heritage Coast Centre there were some spectacular fossils, many of which have been found recently. The Charmouth Dinosaur is very impressive, as is Attenborough's Sea Dragon, an ichthyosaur, which was featured in the BBC documentary 'Attenborough and the Sea Dragon'. We walked along the beach which was cold despite the sun being out but didn't find any fossils. The River Char running down to the sea was full and very fast flowing, probably due to heavy snow falls ten days ago. Apparently, Jane Austin claimed this was her **favourite resort**.   On to Lyme Regis, called 'The Pearl of Dorset' but as the road was narrow and there was no obvious parking, we took some photos of the Cobb and continued on. The Cobb is a protective harbour wall built to form an artificial harbour and a protective breakwater to shelter the town from storms. We carried on to Seaton and then Beer, which has the most westerly white cliffs in Devon. Beer is a very pretty fishing village, with high cliffs and a little harbour well known for its tales of smuggling. It is also famed for its stone, some of which was used in the building of Westminster Abbey.

We checked for messages and got a text from Carol saying she had been offered a job, which she had accepted. We celebrated with rum and raison ice cream, very nice. We then drove on to Sidmouth, where I have visited many times, originally with Nicola, as my aunt had a cottage at Sidbury, which she let out to family. We have also visited here with Norma, Philip, Alison and Bob, my sisters and their husbands, when we stayed in a hotel, for a weekend break. It was sunny for this visit, but when I took Nicola there as a child, it inevitably rained. This time, we took photos of Jacob's Ladder and the high red cliffs, which had had a landfall the previous week. These distinctive red cliffs are the **oldest of the Jurassic coast** and were formed between 250 and 230 million years ago. The red rock indicates the arid conditions of the Triassic geological period. We drove on past Budleigh Salterton, which has lovely, long sweeping beaches and then continued to Exmouth and found our certificated site, which didn't appear to have the advertised toilets and showers. Alan remembers a wooden shack, but I don't think I went there.

73 miles  **Total = 1257**

## THURSDAY 29ᵀᴴ MARCH, 2018

We woke to hear serious rain. Jacob, Alan's third grandchild's, Tenth Birthday, so Alan rang to wish him Happy Birthday. That means that ten years ago we were in India with Norma, Philip, Alison and Bob. Happy memories of a special trip. We left the site in serious rain and drove, in serious rain, down the 'English Riviera'. This is actually a group of villages known collectively as Torbay and spans the towns of Torquay, Paignton and Brixham. At Dawlish there was much landscaping and construction going on, probably repairing damage from recent storms. In 2014 the coastal rail track fell into the sea following tremendous storms and, amazingly, it was repaired in two months. We didn't see much of Torquay or Paignton but headed on to National Trust, Coleton Fishacre, where the sun was shining. At the NT café we had respectively, big, Ham and Mustard Mayo and Cheese and Pickle sandwiches, which were very tasty. We then walked round this impressive Art and Crafts house built in 1920's for the D'Oyly Carte family. The whole, inside and out, is an elegant blend of Art and Crafts, Art Nouveau and Art Deco styles and with the sounds of jazz records playing, it has a carefree and happy atmosphere. Thirty acres of garden surround the house and these flow down steep tiers to the sea far below. I managed to walk down far enough to see the tidal swimming pool that the family had, while Alan sat and enjoyed the wonderful view of Pudcombe Cove. Owing to its position and the high humidity in the garden, there are many tender plants from the Mediterranean, South Africa and New Zealand. It started to rain again as we continued on towards our next site, taking the ferry over the River Dart and arriving to find a pretty site with good views of the sea in the distance.

53 miles **Total = 1300**

## SATURDAY 31ST MARCH, 2018

Easter Saturday. The previous day was Good Friday and it was very cold and wet. We drove into Dartmouth as public transport didn't seem to be running. The centre of Dartmouth was charming, despite the rain, with a large waterfront, lots of inlets and pretty, painted houses rising up the steep sides of the inlets. The whole town is dominated by the Britannia Royal Naval College and the mass of boats in the estuary gave a sense of vibrancy. Hoping that the weather would improve, we crossed the river on a pedestrian ferry and then took the Paignton to Dartmouth Steam Railway train to Paignton. We passed the stop for Agatha Christie's holiday home, 'Greenway', and stayed in the train at Paignton, due to the cold, and waited for it to return to Dartmouth. In the M&S Food Hall, I managed to buy more socks and two new vests! We then went to visit Bayard's Cove and Fort, where Pilgrim Fathers set off in the Mayflower in 1620, after doing repairs following their journey from Southampton. There were 102 pioneers including 36 Puritan refugees. The fort was built in the 16th century to protect the town quay. It controls the narrowest point of the channel at the entrance to Dartmouth harbour. Dartmouth was developed in the Middle Ages because of the deep water anchorage there and it was here in 1147 and again in 1190 that the English contingent departed on crusade. This area of old Dartmouth was fascinating with cobbled, narrow streets and beautifully painted houses. We took a distant photo of Dartmouth Castle which sits opposite Kingswear Castle and between which there is a chain that can be raised to stop enemy ships. Dartmouth Castle was begun in 1380's and about a century later, a gun tower was added, making it the **first fortification in Britain purpose built to mount 'ship sinking' cannon.**

We returned to the camp site where we spent two nights but neither of can really picture it. Today, Saturday, we left in drizzle and headed up and down very steep and narrow roads to NT Overbeck's House and subtropical gardens. I don't think the NT book stated how tricky the drive there could be. Once there, however breathtaking the views, I was thinking of the narrow tracks back down. We briefly looked round the house of this eccentric collector and inventor and saw one of his 'Rejuvenator' machines, which seemed similar to ECT equipment! The gardens were magnificent and it would have been nice to explore them further.

Once down, we drove on to see Burgh Island which is attractively just off the coast but which can be walked to at low tide. Surrounded by beautiful sands, the island hosts an impressive Art Deco hotel, which was frequented by Agatha Christie, Noel Coward and the Duke of Windsor. We continued on through narrow lanes, nearly being scraped by a tractor (driven by a 10 year old?) and got to our mediocre site in Plymouth. Getting here marked the end of our south of England section of the Grand Tour.

62 miles **Total = 1362 miles** (for the south of England from Lowestoft round to Welsh Border).


## SUNDAY 1ST APRIL, 2018

Easter Sunday. We were up early and set off to see Plymouth, which has the **largest Naval Base in Western Europe.** It was very cold but we had an interesting walk and visit. We parked near the Hoe (the definition of which is elusive) and walked towards town passing, first, the red and white stripped Smeaton's Tower lighthouse, **one of the world's most famous lighthouses** built by John Smeaton, in 1759, on the Eddystone Rocks.  Next, we passed a statue of Sir Frances Drake, explorer and local hero.  It is said that he finished his game of bowls before heading out to defeat the Spanish Armada in 1588.  We continued round to the inner harbour of Sutton Pool, where we visited the excellent, and warm, museum and saw the Mayflower Steps, from whence pilgrims set off for America.  2020 marks the 400$^{th}$ anniversary of the sailing of the Mayflower, but as I am writing this in 2020, I know that celebrations will have been cancelled due to Coronavirus.  Overlooking the pool is the 'Plymouth Sea Monster', more commonly called the Barbican Prawn, a weird art work.  It is a combination of an angler fish head, cormorant's feet, the fin of a John Dory, a lobster's claw and the tail of a plesiosaurus.  We then had a chilly boat trip to see various naval ships in the outer harbour.  Back to the site, where it rained all night and I was fearful that the nearby river would overflow and sweep us away.  Fortunately it didn't and we set off for home over a misty and bleak Dartmoor, so we didn't stop.

## WEDNESDAY 4TH JULY, 2018

## WALES

Great to be in Wales and very excited about this next section of our Round Britain Tour.

It had been a stressful few weeks culminating in Alan's visit to meet his cardiac surgeon at Papworth. Mr Ng was pleasant, attentive, confident and very reassuring. Surgery sometime in the next three months, but we both felt more settled having seen the hospital and the surgeon. We drove down to Ickford to see Ruth and Pete and stay in their yard.

It was wonderful to arrive at the Tredegar Country House club site with the sun continuing to shine. Having arrived at midday, we had plenty of time to enjoy our lovely tree lined site and visit NT Tredegar House. Beginning to feel as if we were on holiday and all would be well, we wondered around the grounds and went into the 17th-century mansion, which is an architectural delight and considered the **most significant building of this period in Britain.** This red brick house was home to the Morgans, one of the great Welsh families, later lords of Tredegar, who were great benefactors to the local community and gave land for the construction of the Royal Gwent Hospital. We had a healthy salad supper and an early night, 9pm.

27 miles  **Total = 1389 miles**

## THURSDAY 5TH JULY, 2018

We were up early, it was sunny and it was very hot. We took a bus into Cardiff and went straight to the castle. Located in the heart of the city, Cardiff Castle has a history spanning 2,000 years. The Romans built a fortress here and the Normans built a motte, 40 feet high, and topped with a wooden building, here in the 11th century. Later a 12-sided keep was erected. We climbed to visit this and got fantastic views of Cardiff from the top. We then visited the magnificent Victorian palatial construction, built by the wealthy Bute family. The architect, William Burgess, built this in the style of a medieval castle, with some rooms suggesting part of a fairy tale, and others with intricately painted ceilings, elaborately marbled bathrooms and an impressive clock tower. We then took a City Tour Bus on which we gained additional information. Cardiff Bay was glistening in the sun but before exploring further, we had lunch at Greggs'. A twenty minute boat tour round Cardiff bay was next. The water here is fresh due to the tidal barrier which was started in 1993, following much controversy. As we approached the barrier in the boat we assumed it was sandy but we were informed that it was actually parched grass. Before the construction of the barrier, the bay had one of the world's most expansive tidal ranges of up to 46 feet, rendering it inaccessible for up to 14 hours a day. From the bay we could see the Welsh Assembly building, designed by Richard Rogers and the magnificent Wales Millennium Centre, built from local slate. On the outside, the copper roof/frontage has a bilingual inscription: 'In these stones horizons sing' and 'creating truth like glass from the furnace of inspiration'. Also, on the edge of the bay is the pretty Norwegion church, where Roald Dahl's parents worshiped. The area in front of the centre is called Roald Dahl Plasa.

At the time that we were visiting the city was celebrating 70 years of the NHS, whose creation was largely led by Aneurin Bevan, who was born at Tredegar. We visited his statue and witnessed preparations for celebrations later in the day eg. a large billboard being transported round the city. We had hoped to take the bus back to see the Transporter Bridge at Newport, but were advised that it was 'tricky' by bus, so we got off near our site and went to do some shopping in Asda. We greatly enjoyed our visit to this inspiring and fascinating city, Capital of Wales since 1995.

## FRIDAY 6TH JULY, 2018

We set off at 9.14 am and drove along the A48 to Llantwit Major, where we found St. Illtud's, a dear little church recommended by 'Amazing Places'. This is **one of the oldest Christian sites in the United Kingdom**. St. Illtud came here about the year 500 CE and the present church building is from the 11th century. There are Celtic stones and medieval paintings and some beautiful windows. The symbol of the cross appears in many guises, too, from primitive gouges (stones) to highly elaborate Georgian designs. We also had an interesting tour by a member of the church and bought a booklet about this intriguing place. We continued along the coast, but didn't go down to St. Donat's Castle, despite it being continuously inhabited since it was built in around 1300. We drove along further and visited the viewpoint and SSSI at Merthyr Mawr. It was very hot and the view of the coast was wonderful with the sea a fantastic blue. There is a huge stretch of sandy dunes. The area was a film set for 'Lawrence of Arabia', in 1962.

Here we ate our salads bought in the Llantwit Coop. We joined the M4 to go past Port Talbot with its massive industrial units and chimneys. We got to Swansea and parked safely in Sainsbury's carpark. In its heyday in the 19th century, Swansea was known as 'Copperopolis', Dylan Thomas later called it an 'ugly, lovely town'. We walked to the Dylan Thomas Exhibition Centre, which was very interesting and free. I bought a book of his poetry, which I haven't really got into yet. We walked along the attractive quay to take a photo of Thomas' statue in front of the theatre named after him. We saw the National Waterfront Museum in the Maritime Quarter, but didn't go in. Having returned to the motorhome, we continued onto our next site at Gowerton. As we were in good time, we set off again to drive round the Gower Peninsular. Peaceful and rural, we saw only snatches of the coast.

96 miles **Total = 1485**

## SATURDAY 7TH JULY, 2018

We set off early for Rhossili Beach, said to be one of the **finest unspoilt beaches in Britain**. It is absolutely stunning and deservedly considered the pride of the Gower. It has a perfect, gently arching sandy bay flanked by 250 foot sandstone cliffs and steep grassy slopes of Rhossili Down. We walked towards the head to see the three green humps of Inner Head, Low Neck and Outer Head which snake outwards to form a mile long promontory. The Vikings called it 'wurm' meaning dragon, because of its beast like shape. It was very hot, so we found a café with shade and had very tasty pasties watching hang gliders flying of the cliffs and down to the beach. Very watchable and interesting to have some hang gliders in the café preparing their packs in preparation for the climb and flight. Part of me would love to do that! We went back to the site to watch the England v. Sweden World Cup Quarter final. Nicola sent us a picture of her in her Sweden colours, very brave in Bognor. England won 2:0. We read the papers in the heat and then had a lovely salad for supper.

40 miles **Total = 1525**

## SUNDAY 8TH JULY, 2018

Set off at 9am and headed off towards the Wetland Centre for Wales. However, we were too early and it wasn't open. Also, it would have been too expensive for a short visit, so we continued on to Carmarthen, where we went round and round looking for signs to the famous castle. It eventually dawned on us that we were in the wrong place and that the castle we were looking for was in Caernarfon. Oops, one bit of research that I hadn't done. We had coffee in a layby, relieved that we hadn't stopped and asked anyone, and drove on to Tenby where we would have stopped if we had found parking. We drove along the edge of the proud town walls and past the harbour, which was very pretty. There were flowers everywhere and it was very impressive. We drove on to Manorbier, where there is a lovely old castle and a beautiful beach with, when we were there, a stunning blue sea. The castle, built of quarried limestone, was begun in the 12th century and managed to avoid attack from both the Welsh and Cromwell's armies.

We bought ice creams which melted very quickly as we walked up the cliff path. We got to the Freshwater East Site by 2.30pm and hastened to the sea. It was very hot and we dozed on the beach before having a delightful swim. It was reminiscent of Sardinia, clear water, beautiful sun, very relaxing and therapeutic. Alan said he felt as if he was on holiday – great. He then successfully cooked 'microwave only' salmon meals in the oven, which we ate outside in the sun.

71 miles **Total = 1596**


## MONDAY 9TH JULY, 2018

We left before 9am, and went to NT Stackpole, maybe by a longer route than necessary. However, it is often good to avoid little white roads. This former grand estate stretches down to **some of the best coastline in the world**. We walked to the pretty little quay but didn't continue on the precarious path to Barafundle Bay, said to be **the best beach in Wales**. We headed to Pembroke, birthplace of HenryV11, where Alan saw the splendid castle from the window before we proceeded over the impressive Neyland Bridge. Pembroke Castle stands on a crag overlooking the town and is surrounded by water on three sides. This castle has the distinction of being **the only one in Britain built over a natural cavern**, a large cave known as the Wogan.

We drove on to Marloes via some very small, white roads and continued out to NT Penrhyn, situated at the end of the Marloes peninsular. It was beautiful and very hot. The bay and the islands of Skomer and Skokholm were magical. Graham grew up here, it must have been so hard to leave. We drove back, past Haverford West and up to St. David's. This is **Britain's smallest city**, granted this status due to its holy stature based around its magnificent 12th century cathedral.  We walked down to see this pretty cathedral again but didn't go in again, having visited 9 years previously, when Alan was commanded to take off his sun hat.  Strange the things one remembers.  We bought some delicious rolls on our way back up the hill and ate them in the motorhome before driving on to Fishguard.  This is a busy port but also a pretty seaside town.  We had a short walk in the sun and, before leaving, we stocked up at Tesco Express.

We then drove on to Cardigan and could see its attractive harbour from the coast road.   Just before Aberaeron we found our campsite and later drove into New Quay for a walk and fish and chips, looking over the sea.  New Quay is a bustling seaside harbour which was once a hub for shipbuilders, building ships large enough to sail to the Americas and Australia.  Dylan Thomas lived here with his family in the last years of World War 2 and wrote much of 'Under Milk Wood' here.  The town may have inspired his fictional community of Llareggub.

126 miles  **Total = 1722**


## TUESDAY 10TH JULY, 2018

We left our site just after 9am and drove through Aberaeron, which appeared to be a very pretty village and which is known as 'the jewel of Cardigan Bay'.  Not sure why we didn't stop there as I am sure that Helen, a Welsh friend, recommended it.  We drove along the beautiful coast, which Alan thought the best we had seen so far on our Round Britain Trip.  We accidentally missed the renowned Victorian sea front at Aberystwyth and got caught in the centre of this university town.  We continued on to Machynlleth, said to be the green capital of Wales, along the River Dovey estuary, and on to Aberdovey where we stopped in a lay by near the sea to take photos of this lovely spot.  We drove on to the Afon Mawddach (Maw) estuary. Along one side of the stunning estuary past Arthog, with its landscape that impressed JMW Turner,  and then back along the other side until we came to the outskirts of Barmouth and a prefect parking place overlooking this wonderful stretch of water spanned by the amazing wooden train bridge.  A train obliged by crossing as we ate our cheese and piccalilli sandwiches. An oyster catcher and her chick were scrapping around on the edge of the water below us, a lovely sight and break for us.  We drove through the town and past the Min-y-Mor Hotel, where we had a family holiday when I was 11 years old.  Much of it was familiar, although I didn't recall that the sandy beach was so long and, perhaps, it was more touristy than in 1959. We drove on to our next site at Harlech, which was overlooked by the impressive Harlech Castle, regularly dubbed **the most dramatic in Britain**, sitting high on a 200 foot crag.  We established our place on the camp site which, was expensive and regimented.

It was hot but cloudy as we drove up towards the castle with the road becoming a very steep and narrow lane. Phew!  In 2019, that hill at 40%, was designated **the steepest street in the world**, however, in 2020 New Zealand claimed back that title. Whatever, I was proud of my driving skills. We managed to find a parking place and had a brief visit to the outside of the castle, built within seven years, as one of Edward 1's 'iron ring'.

126 miles  **Total = 1848**

As we had time and no inclination to return early to the campsite, we drove up to the Traeth estuary and then to Blaenou Ffestiniog to see the train. Alan very excited as he loves to see a few steam trains when we are on holiday. This was 'off coast' so the mileage wasn't included. We had a lovely trip into the slatey hills and saw the train with a double fronted engine. We returned for supper in the motorhome, another salad – how healthy we were, and watched the World Cup Semi-Final on television.

## WEDNESDAY 11TH JULY, 2018

Our 20th Wedding Anniversary. Time to celebrate – see later.

We had a good start from Harlech, in cloud but pleasant, and drove on to Portmadog with its lovely harbour and the most visited town on the Llyn peninsular. Nearby Portmerion, the 'weird, intriguing yet magical seaside utopia of heavy Italianate influence' wasn't open as we were too early and we decided not to stay and visit. I visited many years ago with Nicola and had been only marginally impressed, much of it seeming quite weary.

We carried on to Criccieth and saw the castle on a very high mound suggesting the status it once must have had. Nearby, we went to the Lloyd George Museum. This was the home of this WW1 Prime Minister and his uncle's shoemaking business. Lloyd George was the **last Liberal Prime Minister of Britain**. Unfortunately, the museum was closed so we took a photo and continued on to the Llyn peninsular. This was such a pretty peninsular but with lots of narrow lanes. We drove down to Abersoch, which had a charming little harbour even with the tide out, had our coffee in the hills and then continued down to Aberdaron, which we found interesting and charming.  The NT museum, Porth y Swnt, was fascinating, relating history to nature with a modern , artistic and even ethereal feel.  Aberdaron was the leaving place for pilgrims leaving for Bardsey Island, known as the island of 20,000 saints.  In the middle ages, three visits to this island equalled one to Rome.  We saw the pub which dates from the 1300's and which was where the pilgrims were fed before leaving.  We also went to the church, St.Hywyn's, where the pilgrims prayed.  The famed Welsh poet, R. S. Thomas was vicar here from 1954 to 1967.  We had an excellent sandwich on a bench overlooking the beach and watching a group of school children, out for a day, playing various games on the beach.

We returned along the north of the peninsular, past the towering Yr Eifl hills, but we didn't stop as we were getting very low on petrol.  It was in these hills that the tyrant Vortigern was defeated by Ambrosius Aurelianus, in the 5th century.  Ambrosius then became the new leader of the Britons, preparing the way for King Arthur.  Our concerns about petrol continued as we drove along the beautiful North Llyn coast and by this time the oil indicator was flashing red.  Fortunately, we found a garage in the small but special village of Clynnog-fawr.  Alan had trouble checking the oil but was greatly helped by a very helpful young man who happened to be there.  He assisted with oil and coolant and told us that this was a holy village on the North Wales Pilgrim's Way.  This Way stretches for 130 miles from Basingwerk Abbey at Greenfield to Bardsey Island and is regrowing in popularity as a walk.  The garage attendant was also eager to tell us that it was special and pointed out the church of St. Beuno.  The church was on the site of a Celtic Monastery founded by Beuno in the 7th century and was/is an important place for pilgrims heading for Bardsey Island.  It was certainly a blessed place for us.

We drove on more confidently and arrived at the vast Menai Strait. At Caernarfon we had no trouble locating this **grandest and most impressive** of all Welsh castles! This one we had to visit. The building of this magnificent castle was started in 1283 and in 1301 the first Prince of Wales, Edward (later Edward 11) was invested here. This tradition has continued ever since and in 1969, Prince Charles was invested as the current Prince of Wales. The town of Caernarfon was also charming with cobbled streets and remaining town walls. There has been a fort here since Roman times, Segontium, was one of the most famous in Britain. Lloyd George was MP here and there is a fine statue of him.

Getting excited about our forthcoming holiday within our holiday we drove onto the Brittania Bridge and onto Anglesey, noting coastal mileage as we passed. We drove at a good rate to get to our hotel in time to change, have a delicious meal and watch the end of the World Cup Final in our room with a bottle of bubbly provided. Happy 20th Anniversary.

121 miles **Total = 1969**


(**THURSDAY 12TH JULY, 2018** . *Not an official part of our Tour Round Britain, but a delightful break. Anglesey was wonderful and it was sunny. We went to South Stacks and saw Puffins and visited an ancient site near Moelfre and saw 4th century remains of buildings, a chapel and a burial chamber. Back to the hotel for another delicious meal, for me a vegan curry, very good.)*

## FRIDAY 13TH JULY, 2018

After a delicious breakfast, it was back to the motorhome, which felt quite small after our very large hotel room. We drove down to the Menai Strait again, where I wanted to visit NT Plas Newydd, but unfortunately, it didn't open until 11am. I had wanted to see Rex Whistler's huge painting in the dining room, commissioned by the 6th Marquess of Anglesey, in 1930's. It is **Whistler's largest work**, 58 feet long, and features the artist as a gardener.

On to Conwy, a medieval World Heritage Site, where we parked and looked at the castle, which was covered in scaffolding. The castle was built by Henry 1, in 1287, as part of his 'iron ring' to repress rebellious Welsh troops. We admired the Telford Suspension Bridge and had a very pleasant wander along the quay where we saw the **smallest house in Britain**, just six feet wide and ten feet high. The last person to live here was a fisherman, who was 6ft 3in tall. Conwy is the **most complete walled town in Britain** and we found it charming.

We drove over the River Conwy and up the peninsular to the elegant, Victorian Llandudno. This is **Wales' largest seaside resort**, it has the **longest pier in Wales** and **Britain's only cable-hauled tramway**. It also has the largest prehistoric mine in the world.

We viewed the town by driving through it, up to the Great Orme and almost to Little Orme. But it was drizzling, so we drove on seeing some of the Alice in Wonderland statues that are dotted around the town. The real Alice (Liddell) stayed here as a child. In the rain, the north coast road through Colwyn Bay, Rhyl and Prestatyn was rather glum and it was difficult to see the beach or sea due to the caravan parks. A storm arrived as we left Wales and arrived in Chester.  We found our site fairly easily (?) and decided to stay there and visit Chester at the beginning of our next stretch of our Tour Round Britain.

78 miles  **Total = 2047**

## MONDAY, 25TH MARCH, 2019

## NORTH WEST

Wonderful, here we go again after Alan's successful major heart operation last autumn.

We drove up to Chester yesterday and visited the city this morning. Not on the coast but neither of us has been to Chester before and we wanted to see it. Certainly an impressive city with Roman remains, including an amphitheatre and wonderfully well preserved, half-timbered Tudor buildings, mainly in the 'Rows'. We walked some of the walls and through the centre of the city before returning to the motorhome and driving up the Wirral peninsular. We stopped on our way up to visit Ness Botanical Gardens, which were large and impressive on an outcrop above the Dee Estuary and facing the coast of Wales, where we finished our last leg in July 2018. Beautifully landscaped, with some wonderful plants and trees but just a bit early in the year for seeing it at its best.

It was sunny, but the wind was cold as we continued on to our site in Wirral Country Park, on cliffs overlooking the estuary. We walked to the beach but the tide was out so it was not possible to identify the many waders out on the water's edge. We had a very peaceful sit in the sun and began to feel excited and liberated. 'Cooks' Lamb Tagine for supper and then planning for our visit to Liverpool the next day.

16 miles  **Total = 2063**

## TUESDAY 26TH MARCH AND WEDNESDAY 27TH MARCH, 2019

Cities being difficult to access and explore in the motorhome, Tuesday was a day to visit Liverpool by train enabling us to avoid the centre on Wednesday. We drove to Hoylake and took an efficient train, under the Mersey, to Liverpool and arrived by 9.30 am. It was cold so we had a warming coffee at the Beatles Café on the Waterfront and took photos of the large bronze statues of John, Paul, George and Ringo.

We then walked round the Albert Docks, which were beautifully modernised. The five storey warehouses are Britain's **largest group of Grade 1 listed buildings**. We visited the Maritime museum, but unfortunately, we found the Slavery Section rather poor as it appeared to underplay the impact of Liverpool's role in slavery. However, the Titanic Section was quite interesting. Alan took a photo of me with a Billy Fury Statue but we then decided to go on a City Tour Bus, hoping it would be warmer. We saw the Cavern and went into the Philharmonic Dining Rooms for lunch. This elegant late Victorian building was designed to be reminiscent of the grand interior of a transatlantic liner. There are carved and glazed mahogany partitions which radiate from the mosaic-faced bar and the ceiling has semi nude caryatids. Instruments, once used in the orchestra and copper relief panels of musicians are numerous. Alan was much impressed by the fancy tilework and red marble fittings in the Gents. We then walked to the Metropolitan Cathedral, which was stunning. The Catholic Diocese of Liverpool was established in 1850, but it wasn't until 1933 that the foundation stone for this building was laid. It is on the site of the former Workhouse but building was delayed by the outbreak of WW11 and then by escalating costs. A new design was made by Frederick Gibberd and work was completed in 1967. There is a vast circular inner space which seats 2,300 people, arranged around a central sanctuary and High Alter.

The walls are covered with embroidered hangings and the side chapels contain works of art and devotion by contemporary artists. We next visited the Anglican Cathedral which was, in contrast, old and dark.

It was unfortunate that we didn't go to the Walker Art Gallery, which was showing the work of architect, designer and artist Charles Rennie Mackintosh. Fish and chips were being sold on site that evening, so, of course, we took advantage of this.

The next day, Wednesday, we continued round the Wirral, up to New Brighton and down the other side along the Mersey. At Ellesmere Port we visited the National Waterways Museum, which was on the Shropshire Union Canal with the beginning of the Manchester Ship Canal behind. It contains the **world's largest collection of inland waterways craft**, from coracles to narrow boats. Among the more unusual vessels is an ice boat, with a handrail stretching centrally from bow to stern for those on board to grasp as they rocked the hull to break frozen water. There is a historic engine collection and much information about the mechanics and functioning of this port. Not far from the end of the peninsular is NT Speke Hall, a black and white, Tudor style building built 500 years ago on the site of a medieval manor house. It was restored in Victorian times and has many Arts and Crafts features including William Morris wallpaper.

Going up the other side of the Mersey we decided to take the ring road round Liverpool, having visited the day before, but somehow ended up back on the waterfront, driving past the Liver Building again.

We had a slow and journey through Bootle and had some confusion finding Crosby beach. However we got there and had a lovely walk viewing Antony Gormley's artwork 'Another Place', comprising 100 life sized cast iron figures stretching a kilometre out to sea. It was cold but sunny and very well worth seeing. We drove just a bit further to get to Formby beach, which was again, good to see. Fabulous sand dunes and a stunning beach, but we didn't get sight of any of the resident red squirrels. We arrived at Southport site at 5.15 and Alan prepared our Cook's supper of Pork in Mustard sauce, very good.

109 miles = **Total 2172**

## THURSDAY 28TH MARCH, 2019

Quite an early start, having been woken by a noisy flight of geese overhead and the cheerful song of the thrush – could it be the same one that we heard at previous two sites! We left at 8.30am and, so, were too early to visit RSPB Leighton Moss, which is home to **Britain's largest concentration of breeding bitterns**. We progressed on to Preston where we could see an ornate tower on the church, and then continued on to Lytham and Lytham St. Annes, where we passed the impressive grade 11 listed church, The White church, which is also said to be beautiful inside. On into Blackpool, often considered **Britain's gaudiest and craziest seaside resort**, passing the Big Dipper, **the tallest roller coaster in the UK** which reaches speeds of 87mph!! We parked on the front and had coffee before undertaking the long walk along the promenade to the Tower, built in 1894 to imitate the Eiffel Tower in Paris. When it was opened it was the tallest man made structure in the British Empire.

Up to the **most spectacular ballroom in the UK,** where several couples were dancing, probably regulars, familiar with each other and with the organist, and dressed variously in psychedelic leggings, gold lame and gold shoes. I was wearing my walking boots so we just watched for a while but didn't take part. It is a wonderful building with beautiful brickwork and tiling. We walked back looking at the massive sandy beach although the sea was a long way out. So far on this trip, we had hardly seen the sea as it was always out when we went near to an estuary or beach.

It was out of season but still a slow drive north along the coast to Fleetwood, where we found a small Asda for inviting panini and provisions. We drove on and through Lancaster with its elegant buildings and University, and on to Morecombe. Here was a very basic site but good for walking to the Midland Hotel for our meal, a 70th Birthday treat for me from Ruth and Pete. We dressed up and had a chilly walk to the hotel but got a great table overlooking the sea, just in time for the sun to appear and provide a beautiful mottled sun set over Morecombe Bay. This elegant art-deco hotel was used in a Poirot film in 1990. We had a delicious meal and toasted Ruth and Pete for giving us such a lovely treat.

83 miles = **2252 miles**

## FRIDAY 29TH MARCH, 2019

We left at 9.30 and drove along Morecombe sea front and saw the Eric Morecombe statue. We then drove on to the delightful RSPB Leighton Marsh and although we couldn't stop long, had a pleasant walk and identified a Marsh Tit and a Nuthatch. Back on the road, we drove round the River Kent Estuary and on to Grange Over Sands and Kents Bank which are on the northern side of Morecombe Bay. This massive bay is 10 miles wide and has an area of 120 square miles. There is an ancient right of way across the bay but only the foolhardy would risk the tide and attempt to cross without the official Queen's Guide.

North again and then south to Ulverston, where we bought salad lunches at the supermarket over looked by the Barrow Monument, which looks like a lighthouse high on a hill behind the town. It was designed to look like the Eddystone Lighthouse, but has never had a functional light, and it commemorates Sir John Barrow, a founder member of the Royal Geographical Society. We drove further south past Bardsea and Baycliff, which has a stunning wide view of Morecombe Bay. From Rampside we drove onto Roa Island with a view of Piel castle (EH), a 14$^{th}$ century fortress, accessible only by boat, and built as a refuge from pirates and Scots raiders. We crossed the deep water channel to the Walney Island and looked over to Barrow in Furness, where the Vickers shipyard has been building warships since 1896. We drove back and through the massive industrial area of Barrow, with Alan noting the well barricaded BAE Systems complex and commenting on their production of high tech weapons etc. We took a waggly road north and then went south again to Millom passing the fascinating 'Ancient Village of Holy Trinity', which still functions as an Anglican church. (Strangely, this is not on the map and I can't find it on Google).  We drove on northwest as near to the coast as possible to get to our campsite in a field.  It was very rural, overlooking Eskdale Estuary with views of the train bridge for the little Carlisle to Barrow Railway.  Alan rang Jacob to wish him a Happy 11th Birthday and they had a good little chat.  This should have been Brexit Day!  We didn't want it anyway and it was looking like an embarrassing mess!  We got on with cooking a curry and opening a bottle of wine.

105 miles = **Total 2357 miles**

## SATURDAY 30TH MARCH, 2019

Set off from the field at about 10am, having used the messy farm buildings for toilet only.  We parked in Ravenglass where we viewed the Caravan Club site from the gate.  We might have stayed there but hadn't wanted to stay two nights, a Caravan Club requirement.  We went to the station for the Ravenglass and Eskdale Railway and saw the locomotive getting up steam ready for its journey up to Muncaster.  This popular tourist attraction was fairly full and Alan would have liked to join the cheerful passengers on their journey.  This narrow gauge railway was opened in 1875 to carry iron ore from Boot to Ravenglass.  It was originally 3ft gauge but was converted to 15in gauge in 1915.  After seeing the train leave the station we walked along a track to visit the EH Ravenglass Roman Bath House.  This is **one of the tallest surviving Roman structures in northern Britain**, with the walls standing 4 metres high, complete with remains of plasterwork and elegant niches for statues.  This bath house serves the Ravenglass Roman fort, which guarded a useful harbour and was garrisoned by troops from Hadrian's fleet. Small, but interesting.

We then continued driving north, leaving the coast for a while but seeing Sellafield in the distance. This large multi-function nuclear site, close to Seascale, is a former nuclear power generating site but is now used for nuclear fuel reprocessing, nuclear waste storage and nuclear decommissioning. **It is Europe's largest nuclear site and has the most diverse range of nuclear facilities in the world situated on a single site.**

On to St. Bees where we had to stop to reminisce about the first day of our honeymoon, twenty one years before. The Wainwright Coast to Coast Walk is 182 miles long and it passes through three contrasting national parks: the Lake District, the Yorkshire Dales and the North York Moors national Parks. It was one of the best holidays we have had even though I ended up with lobar pneumonia. As we did when doing the walk, we picked up pebbles to take to Robin's Hood Bay when we got there on our journey round the coast. We drove on to Whitehaven which continues to be a working port and which has some very elegant Georgian buildings remaining from when Whitehaven was the most important British port after London. In 1778, the **last invasion of the British mainland** took place here, when American revolutionaries tried and failed to attack the merchant fleet docked in the harbour.

We then had a long drive further north via Workington and Maryport, which has a Roman Fort which we didn't visit. Next was a drive up a beautiful coast road towards Silloth, but we had to turn back as the road was closed. We took a diagonal across to near the Solway Firth and could have taken a scenic coastal route along the firth but the navigator said there wasn't one. We should have known, as we had walked on a road track close to the water when completing the Hadrian's Wall Walk a few years ago.

However, as a result, we arrived early, at 3.30, to a horrid, soulless, inland site, probably the worst we have been on.

99miles **Total = 2456**

## SUNDAY 31ST MARCH, 2019

## SCOTLAND

A lovely day ending on the edge of a beautiful sea loch harbour. The day started cold and neither of us could face going to the cold leaking showers, so we set off early for the border and Gretna Green. It was too early to visit the Blacksmith's shop where the weddings take place but did take the coastal road to Caerlaverock (rock of the skylark), where we visited a fabulous Waterfowl and Wildlife Trust Centre (WWT). There were masses of noisy Whooper swans, just leaving for Iceland and great flocks of Barnacle geese, circling and landing but not quite ready to leave for Svalbad. Fabulous tufted ducks and teal all very close to the Peter Scot viewing building. We walked down to the Solway Firth and looked across to where we could have driven the day before. Beautiful. Then we drove on to Caerlaverock Castle, which is an impressive 13th century triangular building with a water filled moat. It would have been expensive to visit, so we took a photo and continued on our way. We were now on the 'Burn's Heritage Route' and we drove on to Dumfries but didn't visit the town again, having been there a few years before. Now really experiencing the inlets and ruggedness of the Scottish coast, we drove due south, still bordering the Solway Firth, to Sweetheart Abbey, by which we were fascinated when we visited before.

It looked wonderful in the sun. This Cistercian Abbey was founded in 1273 by Devorgilla, Lady of Galloway and wife of John Balliol, an Anglo-Norman baron. He was only 18 and she only 13 when they married. After he died in 1268 she carried his heart in a casket with her for 20 years until she died, and then she and her husband's heart were buried in front of the high alter of the abbey church.

Further down the coast we passed the home of John Paul Jones who started the American navy. Then north again and south again and round to Kirkcudbright, which is known as the 'Artist's Town', a very pretty harbour town. The street plan is medieval and the castle ruin at its heart dates from the 16th century. The town's fame as a centre for painters dates from 1901, when the artist E A Hornel settled here. It is said that local residents asked Hornel for advice when painting the outside of their houses and this explains the harmonious shades seen in the High Street. The town was full of galleries, closed as it was a Sunday, but one of them was being set up for an exhibition starting the next day and they allowed us to go in for a preview. Interesting, but expensive, so we were not inclined to buy. Next we drove north again round Wigtown Bay and past the remains of Cardoness Castle, which was once a sturdy fortress on the Cliffside above the bay. Then we drove south again to Wigtown, 'The Book Town', which again, as it was Sunday was, unfortunately closed. I could have spent some serious time there. We continued on to Garlieston site, which we thought the best Motor Home or Caravan Club site yet visited. It was situated on the edge of the estuary and we had a wonderful view from our pitch, the sun was shining, it was warm and we each had a delicious 'Cream of Gallaway' ice cream, with plans to eat at the Harbour Inn in the evening. Great.

128 miles **Total = 2584**

## MONDAY 1ST APRIL, 2019

Another great day, despite dismal weather. The tide came in at Garieston and we saw several redshanks and oyster catchers on the beach before leaving. Continuing on the Solway Firth Heritage Trail, which stretches from near Gretna to Stranraer, we drove south to the Isle of Whithorn, to see the ruins of St. Ninian's Chapel. This is **Scotland's earliest recorded Christian settlement.** St. Ninian was a locally born missionary who travelled to Rome in the 4$^{th}$ century. He was ordained by the pope and given the task of spreading Christianity to western Britain. The 'Candida Casa' or White House, was his first church and priory, built in AD 397, and it gave rise to the name of the village. The present ruins date from the 12$^{th}$ century, but there are remains and fragments of stained glass which date from 500, showing Whithorn to be a significant place of pilgrimage for the Irish, Northumbrians, Vikings, Anglo-Normans and Scottish settlers. We had a chilly but very interesting walk through the town. There was, then, a long drive to the hammerhead shaped Rhins of Gallaway and down to the **Mull of Galloway, the most southerly point of Scotland**. The weather was poor but it is a stunning place and has a super café, where we had lunch. We then drove up the coast to pretty Logan Bay but we didn't visit the renowned Logan Botanical Garden although we could see many palm trees from the road. We continued to Portpatrick, which was to runaway Irish couples what Gretna was to eloping English lovers. This is Scotland's closest point to Ireland and it was a busy port for British Troops, settlers and travellers.

Across the Rhinn and in a more sheltered position is the busy port and ferry terminal of Stranraer, which we passed through before heading north again. We could see the crag of Ailsa

Craig through the mist and on land passed the showy, American, Trumpian, Turnberry Golf Club and complex. What a blot on the landscape. We easily found the delightful Culzean site, in the grounds of Culzean castle and which was that day, just opening for the season. The staff were very welcoming and excited about the new season. We chose a spot on the edge of the site where we had a fantastic view across Culzean Bay and the Firth of Clyde to Arran. Over the next couple of days as the light changed we took several photos of this view.

135 miles   **Total = 2719**


## TUESDAY 2ND APRIL, 2019

We stayed close to the site and explored Culzean Castle and grounds. Culzean is the National Trust for Scotland's most popular property. Architect Robert Adam designed this golden stone castle for the Kennedy family in the late 1700's. It is set right on the edge of cliffs in 563 lush green acres of wild gardens and woodland. We wondered around the house and up the famed graceful oval staircase to get even better views of the coast. We enjoyed the walled gardens and walked through some of the wonderful parkland. A very relaxing day.

## WEDNESDAY 3RD APRIL, 2019

A storm brewed up over night and the sea was very rough in the morning and it was very cold. We left just before some 'wintery storms' began and we witnessed some very lively seas in the bays. On the A719 to Ayr is the Electric Brae, an optical illusion, where due to the configuration on either side of the road, it looks as if the slope is going in the opposite direction. We travelled on to Ayr but, in the rain, we admired some large houses but didn't find anywhere to stop. The town is famed for having been Robert Burns' birthplace, but it was also once Scotland's leading west coast harbour, until it was overtaken by Glasgow. In 1315, Robert the Bruce (as Bruce was my maiden name, I wonder if he was a distant relative) held a parliament here and later Cromwell made Ayr his centre of government for much of Scotland. In warmer weather, it could have been an interesting place to visit.

We drove on through Prestwick and on to Troon, home of Open Golf, passing numerous golf clubs all along the coast. This coast was also busy with Caledonian Mc Brayne ferries going out and back across the Firth of Clyde. We stopped for lunch just outside Fairlie and watched a little ferry busying to and fro across to the small island of Great Cumbrae. Largs looked quite smart and appeared to have the most expensive golf clubs. The Battle of Largs, in 1263, had no clear winner but it was the **last time that the Vikings invaded Scotland**.

All along this coast there were little ports with loads of sailing yachts and Gourlock seemed to have a particularly large number of large masts. Clearly the place for golf or sailing. Turning east towards Glasgow we passed Greenock, whose prosperity was built on refining sugar and weaving cotton. It was also a centre for shipbuilding and the **terminus of the world's first passenger**

**steamship** service. It now welcomes cruise ships and tourists at its ocean terminal. Along the side of the Clyde, on the A8, were many wharfs some in use but some quite derelict. We had decided to stay at the airport Travelodge so that we could visit Glasgow by bus. Entering the airport grounds was strange and finding the Travelodge a bit tricky but we got there and it was fine.

Mileage taken at the Erskine bridge was 91 miles so **Total = 2810**

## THURSDAY 4TH APRIL, 2019

A very interesting day in Glasgow, which, although not on the coast, really needed a visit. We walked much and used the City Tour Bus to visit many of the highlights. Unfortunately not able to see Caroline, a niece of mine, and her family this time, but we had plans for our next visit in May. I particularly liked the Rennie Mackintosh features and Alan really enjoyed the Riverside Museum, which houses historic vehicles, engines, motorbikes and transport paraphernalia. We both greatly enjoyed the Kelvingrove Art Gallery and Museum and loved seeing 'Dippy' the dinosaur on loan from the Natural History Museum in London. Alan hadn't seen it before and was quite impressed. A lovely day, before setting out for home via Mansfield Premier Inn to see Carol and family for dinner the next day.

## THURSDAY 9TH MAY, 2019

It was so exciting to be off on this stretch of our Round Britain Tour. Exciting because it was my beloved Scotland, exciting because it was to be our longest time away and excited because there was to be so much to see and the weather forecast was good. It is also amazingly exciting to start writing about this part of our Tour.

We set off on Tuesday 7th and drove up to Yorkshire to stay at a B&B in Danby Wiske, that we had visited when walking the Coast to Coast. Alan has a fondness for this village as his aunt spent some time there during the war and spoke of it with affection. The White Swan is very much a walkers' pub and basic, but it was fun to visit it again and reminisce. On the 8th, we set off, after a good pub breakfast, along the scenic A66 and headed north for Glasgow. We found the Premier Inn in Bearsden quite easily and then walked to have a delightful meeting up and meal with Caroline and family. They were all great company and it was a pleasure to visit their home.

We set off at 9.30 and took our mileage at the Erskine Bridge, then had some problems finding the A814 coastal road. We eventually got the right junction off the dual carriageway and drove to Dumbarton on the north side of the Firth of Clyde. This delightful place was once **one of the most important places in Scotland** and the proud castle stands high on Dumbarton Rock (a 250 foot volcanic plug) overlooking the Clyde and visible from miles away. Between the 5th and 9th centuries, Dumbarton was the seat of a powerful British kingdom that dominated much of southern Scotland. It then became the seat of Scottish kings until 1018, when Dunfermline became the capital. In the 19th century, Dumbarton was one of the world's greatest ship building centres, giving birth to vessels such as the clipper 'Cutty Sark' and the 'Sir

Walter Scott', which still carries passengers on Loch Lomond.

We had a pleasant walk looking at the scenery, the castle and the wide Clyde. We drove on to Helensburgh, which is where Graham was born, a pretty town at the beginning of the sea loch, Loch Gare. There is a vast, very well protected naval base here with barriers extending miles along the road. We were now on the Route of the Scottish Sealochs, one of Scotland's most popular driving routes. The sun was shining, it was warm and it was beautiful. The actual coast is sometimes difficult to ascertain but we did our best, driving miles north, then south, east and west to keep as closely as possible, but realistically to our plans. We drove along the side of Gare Loch and then to Loch Long, where we stopped at Portincaple for coffee and to view a large Russian vessel at the Finnort Ocean Terminal, an oil terminal and also well protected.

There being no roads on the other side of the loch, from Tarbet we crossed, past Rest and Be Thankful to Loch Fyne and Cairndow. Rest and be Thankful are the words inscribed on a stone at a high point on the A83, site of an old military road. We couldn't stop at every place of interest, so continued on. It was beautiful wherever we looked and it was such a joy to be there. We drove down the side of Holy Loch to Dunoon, still on the Firth of Clyde. Holy Loch is so called from the 6$^{th}$ century, when St. Munn landed there after leaving Ireland. We stopped for lunch, a roll from the café, only a couple of miles across the water to where we were a month before when approaching Glasgow!

As all roads were dead ends, we crossed the peninsular on single track roads, with a few passing places, and enjoyed the picturesque scenery. Up the side of Loch Fyne again, and then south again down the other side, to go through Inveraray. This interesting town is a significant junction for roads to the west of Scotland and the Western Isles and we have been through it several times.  It was once the capital of Argyll and the castle is a monument to the political and military skills of the Campbell's and the Inveraray Jail is the town's former courthouse, now a museum with some nasty examples of punitive punishments.  A little further south on Loch Fyne is the famous Loch Fyne Oyster Bar and Seafood Centre.  We had to stop!  It was fascinating but expensive and we would have bought more if we could have trusted the motorhome's small freezer.  However, we were very satisfied with the salmon rolls we bought and the pâté for later.

On our way south we visited Crarae Gardens, which specialised in rhododendrons and azaleas and it was the perfect time of year to visit with spectacular colours everywhere we looked.  'Rooted in earth, nourished by water, fed by the sun's fire …. Moving in wind and growing towards the sky.'  The elements are the essence of the spirit of the garden created by Captain George Campbell as he transformed a highland glen into a Himalayan gorge in 1925.  It includes a Neolithic chambered cairn (2500 BC) and is a wonderful place to visit.

It was then a long way south via Lochgilphead to Tarbert, which had a very pretty harbour but which was very busy.  We wanted to find our site, so continued on and found the site unfinished!  We found a notice which advised us to go back to another site to collect keys and check in, which we did.  Returning, there were only two other motorhomes on the unfinished site, near the road but overlooking Loch Tarbert and with good facilities.  A bit sparse but lovely scenery.

167 miles  **Total = 2977**

## FRIDAY 10TH MAY, 2019

A day marked by more bluebells and azalias together with wonderful sunshine. We left the site at 9.30 and started down the west coast of Kintyre seeing Islay, Gigha and eventually Northern Ireland out at sea. It was stunning scenery and a wonderful drive all the way to Campbeltown. There is a massive, apparently impenetrable rock/headland at the end of the peninsular which gives the sense of the mull, guess what we were singing!

We did our shopping in the co-op and returned up the east of Kintyre with good views of Arran. To think, we had been viewing the other side of Arran from Culzean, just about a month ago, on our last trip. This road was bendy and narrow with passing places. We had our coffee on the edge of the water, looking over the sea. We then crossed back over the peninsular, through Tarbert again and up to Lochgilphead again. Unfortunately, I forgot that I had wanted to drive along the Crinan Canal and, so, instead we continued on the A816 to Kilmartin. Kilmartin was interesting and a delightful place to visit. First we overshot the village and had our Loch Fyne salmon pâté in a country carpark with great views of Carnasserie Castle, a 16$^{th}$ century fortified house.

The whole area around Kilmartin is littered with piles of boulders, the remains of burial cairns dating from around 3000 BC. These, together with stone circles, tombs and shrines and enigmatic carvings on the rock faces above appear haunted by the spirits of the early inhabitants. The oldest monuments were built by Neolithic farmers who settled here 6000 years ago. The museum was very interesting and the ice creams delicious.

We were then expecting a long journey up to Oban, but this became longer and very worrying when there was an accident on the main road and we were diverted to a narrow hill road/track, which was single width with few passing places, leading to much queuing of traffic. Not good for me or the motorhome! However, we got to Oban, filled up with fuel and continued on to Onich, to arrive just before 6pm. What a shame, we would have loved to explore this excellent site and its surroundings. It was large but had wonderful views over Loch Linnhe. It was still sunny and warm but there were clouds up over Glen Coe and over Ben Nevis, which we climbed in very hot sun in 2000.

166 miles  **Total = 3143**

## SATURDAY 11TH MAY, 2019

We set off from Bunree site in good time, excited by the prospect of again visiting Ardnamurchan Point, **the most westerly point of main land Britain**. We had arrived there on a ferry from Mull, in 2012, and had loved it. So, we continued north to Fort William, another significant hub on the west coast, in the shadow of Ben Nevis. The original fort was knocked down in 1864 to make space for a train station. We have visited a few times, most notably when we completed the West Highland Way walk. From here we headed west with Ben Nevis looking splendid, and drove through Glenfinnan, noting the site which we would be returning to that night. As we passed, we could see the Glenfinnan monument, marking the place where Prince Charles Edward Stuart raised the Jacobite standard, rallying a call for his father's claim to the throne of Scotland. It was the start of the Stuart's final attempt to regain the British throne, which would end the following year in disaster at Culloden.

As we drove onto the Ardnamurchan, there was a loud 'Wow' from the passenger seat as Alan became mesmerised by the incredibly beautiful view over the Sound of Arisaig. As we passed Arisaig and Salan, the road became increasingly narrow and, although there were many passing places, the motorhome was not liking the stopping and starting. There seemed to be lots of vehicles coming in the opposite direction, which made us think that a ferry must have come in from Mull. Soon an 'engine alert' light came on and we were worried.

Fortunately, we managed to get to the RSPB Glenborrodale parking place, where we stopped and took stock. Alan checked water, oil etc and all seemed fine, but as it was nearing midday on Saturday, we decided to ring Green Flag. A local garage soon contacted us and half an hour later a mechanic arrived with a low loader, surely not necessary? But, he took us to his garage at Acharacle, where they worked hopefully on the motorhome before announcing, at 3.30pm, that we needed to go to a Fiat Dealer in Inverness. We were down hearted but accepted the inevitable and quite enjoyed it in the cab of this monstrous transporter. We rang the site at Culloden and they managed to fit us in for two nights, so it was there that we arrived at 7.59pm after a worrying but at times amusing day. Didn't check mileage, so some tweeking and calculating to do later.

## SUNDAY 12TH MAY, 2019

We had selected a pitch at the back of the site, beside a field of sheep, so we had a delightfully restful day in the sun, watching the sheep and lambs. Some things are meant to be. We could have walked to the Culloden Battlefield, but having been told that it was a field and that much of it could be seen from the road we followed our instincts and enjoyed the peace and rest of our privileged position. The day ended with fish and chips from a visiting mobile 'Chippie', just right.

## MONDAY 13TH MAY, 2019

Eager to be back on the road, we were up at 6.15am and at the Fiat Garage by 8am. By 10am, we were informed that they needed a part, which wouldn't arrive until the next day. So, back to the site with our ailing motorhome to be first in the queue at 12md to bagsy the pitch 'with a view', which we achieved. Don't know what we would have done if the site had been fully booked. So, another charming day, watching the shepherd and his wife arrive early and late to inspect their flock and the sheep and lambs gently grazing.

## TUESDAY 14TH MAY, 2019

Up early again to get to the garage for 8am, before the staff, hopeful that the part had arrived and that it wouldn't take longer than the one hour advised, to fit. Several cups of delicious coffee and two enormous and very tasty rolls later, we were told, at 2pm, that the motorhome was fit to drive. Eureka, but where to go? Fortunately, we had been considering this and had worked on possible destinations, seriously hoping that we would not have to reschedule any more sites. I was determined to get back to where we had left the coast, so that there were no gaps in our TRB with the motorhome.

We rang and managed to get a place reserved at Gairloch and told them that we would be late arrivals, so off we went, back down the side of a beautiful Loch Ness and back to the west coast , noting mileage as we got back on track and having a quick 'wee and tea' overlooking the much photographed Eilean Donan Castle. There has been a fortification here since the 13th century, although the present castle is the result of restoration in the early 1900's. With brooding hills around, this romantic castle sits at the point where three sea lochs meet: Loch Alsh, Loch Duich and Loch Long.

This is a stunning part of the world, along the Wester Ross Coastal Road, and to make haste without further stopping was sad but necessary in the circumstances. Missing the Applecross peninsular had been decided on previously, despite Caroline's amused encouragement that we take the risk. We arrived at the delightful but unwieldy Gairloch site in time for Alan to cook our pre-prepared curry, while I calculated our mileage. I worked it out as 218 since leaving Bunree, on Loch Linnhe, not counting the detour.

**Total = 3361**

## WEDNESDAY 15TH MAY, 2019

Woke early and excited soon after 6am and had showered by 6.30 am. Eggs for breakfast, and then a lovely walk on the sandy beach of Gairloch's wide and beautiful sandy bay. We paddled in the fairly warm sea by 9am and felt cheered and ready to resume our tour. We set off driving by azure seas, the sight of which we followed for most of the day. We didn't visit Gairloch's Heritage Museum, but continued up to NTS Inverewe Gardens, which are **one of the most spectacular gardens in Scotland,** especially in the sun. There were wild, blousy rhododendrons in golds, pinks, reds and white all at their best. Also, there were exotic, and some subtropical, trees and shrubs flourishing in the unique microclimate right on the edge of Loch Ewe. The walled garden had neat rows of flowers and vegetables and a stunning view over the bay. What a treat.

We continued our journey north, east, south and then north again along this most beautiful of coasts. We wanted to keep as close to the coast as possible but also, sincerely wanted to avoid the narrow single track roads, as we didn't want the motorhome upset again. Ullapool looked very pretty glimmering in the sun, as we approached and we stopped in the town to stock up at Tesco's and to buy Alan some shorts at a sports shop. We continued and had lunch near Ardmair overlooking the shining sea.

Our drive up to Scourie did include some narrow roads but it was lovely and the site was stunning, on the edge of Scourie Bay. Our pitch was ' right on the edge' and had a magnificent view toward Handa. We still can't decide if this place matched or exceeded our best ever site on Mull, a few years previously. The coast from here up to Cape Wrath is made mainly of **Lewisian gneiss, one of the oldest rocks in Great Britain** and of astounding antiquity, with rocks at Scourie being dated as nearly 3,000 million years old. **Scotland's first Geopark**, a community and cultural enterprise based on the region's geological heritage, covers the area. Scourie was the main settlement of the MacKay clan until it was sold to the Duke of Sutherland, one of the landowners **most active in the notorious Highland clearances**, compelling many local people to emigrate to Canada, Nova Scotia or Australia.

We walked from the site, along the bay, taking it all in and looking at the many birds. We identified goldfinch, linnets, a great grey shrike, meadow pippits and oyster catchers (we think) and returned to have a fish and chip super in the café before watching a stunning sunset over Handa. Wow! My spirits still zoom up, just to recall the beauty.

103 miles   **Total = 3464**


## THURSDAY 16TH MAY, 2019

Our original schedule had been for two nights at Scourie, but one was excellent and we were very relieved to be back on schedule with, hopefully, no more rebooking. We were up at 6.30am, with a view to visiting Handa. When we went on an expedition ship round the Outer Hebrides, a few years ago, we had great weather and even got to visit St. Kilda, but a storm stopped us getting to Handa, so we were eager to get there this time.

However, the little ferry was late and the skipper told us that we would need time and energy to do the strenuous climb. We felt this wasn't for us and we had a long journey planned, so we returned to our route and stopped for coffee in a peaceful glen, passing the peninsular on which Cape Wrath stands. It was a beautiful spot in the sun and it was very warm. Another 'special moment', much helped by seeing a Golden Eagle soaring above us. We wanted to stay longer to just enjoy the experience but we had a plan to follow.

The next stretch, up the side of the Kyle of Durness, brings tears to my eyes to recall and no good enough words to describe. Picture perfect seas in amazing shades of blue and turquoise and sands in pinks and yellows, it was breath taking and I had to stop and just look, and try to take it in.

We visited the Balnakeil Craft Village, established in 1964 on the site of an old radar station and which is situated near the village of Durness. It is home to a range of local artists and businesses and I particularly wanted to see the gallery of Ishbel Macdonald, whose work I had seen flyers for. Her work is fantastic and very representative of this locality in which she works, with soaring waves and subtle colours reflecting the landscape. I particularly liked one painting, 'Sango Bay', costing £400, and was very tempted but, despite Ishbel offering to have it sent home for us, I decided not to buy. Just recently, however, we rang and tried to purchase a painting from Ishbel but the one we wanted had been sold, however, we bought three prints from her instead, and we are very pleased with them. **Geographically, as the crow flies, this area is the furthest from our home in Suffolk**.

Leaving this beautiful place, we then had a long drive along the awesome north coast of Scotland and Britain. It may appear to be a straight run along the top on maps, but the coast undulates, in and out of delightful sandy coves, has high cliffs in places and has no road in others, requiring you to drive inland, again often, on single track roads. Going predominantly east, but also south and north at times we set off with John O'Groats as our destination. We had done so much already that day, that visiting Smoo Cave just wasn't possible. I hadn't visited it with Nicola either when we took this journey back in the 1980's, but I am a bit dubious about visiting caves. Viking raiders used this one when they launched raids along the north coast, but long before that it was actually created by a fault in limestone layers deposited around 500 million years ago. Apparently, inside the huge sea cave there is a floor of debris left by prehistoric inhabitants. As we progressed eastwards, Alan noticed smoke rising off a moorland hill, which we soon realised was the heath fire mentioned on the front pages of some of the Scottish newspapers.

Further on, we could see that the wind was carrying the smoke eastwards and we hoped that our destination would be safe. The nearer we got, we could see how widespread the fires were. The hill appeared to be steaming and the surrounding moor was covered with smaller smoky fires which eventually crossed the road. The fire service dealt with this by closing the road, allowing only single convoys of six cars to go through with fire trucks at the front and back, first in one direction and then the other. The peat is known to burn for days once alight and the fires were clearly well established and smouldering on the edge of the tarmac producing dense and smelly smoke.

Having come through that, we had lunch near Strathnaver Museum, Bettyhill, the grounds of which we visited briefly in order to see a Pictish cross. We have a friend who once lived at Bettyhill and when she mentioned it, I couldn't remember the place, now I can, so thanks to Sheila for bringing it to my attention.

We passed the nuclear sites at Dounreay. Most of the facilities there are now being decommissioned.  This site will enter an interim care and surveillance state in 2036, and not become a brownfield site for other uses until 2336!   And they are thinking to extend Sizewell!!

We continued on to Dunnet Head, another stunning spot and a real achievement for us, as it is **Britain's Northernmost Point**. We had now been East, South, West and North on our RBT. It was wickedly windy at Dunnet Head, but it was beautiful with sheer, rocky cliffs and an attractive lighthouse.  We drove to our site for the night at John O'Groats, just past the 'last house'.  Our pitch was about 20 yards from the cliff edge with unbelievable views across the sea to Stroma and the Orkney Islands.  When we were last here, it was to cross to the Orkneys, which we did on a still and scorching hot day, in 2000.  This time John O'Groats was windy and cold and it was an effort to visit the touristy sign post which was our photographic evidence of having been there.   So, all south from here! Emmerdale Beef Casserole for dinner - tasty.

135 miles  **Total = 3598**

## FRIDAY 17TH MAY, 2019

We had a good sleep and when we woke at 7am, the sea was calmer and the view was still splendid.  I had a strange sense of anti-climax, having got to the most northerly point, was it just downhill to home?  No! So much more to see. We were off the site by 9.30 am and headed towards Wick, which in 1850's was Europe's busiest herring port, with a fleet of 1,100 boats.  We got provisions at Tesco's, which was situated on high ground with an amazing view, must get the supermarket with the best view award, if there is one.  There was big, rolling countryside and steep cliffs. We had lunch at Dunrobin Castle carpark, and then went round the castle and viewed the Versailles inspired gardens from the terrace. This was the seat of the Dukes of Sutherland and exemplifies the wealth and privilege of aristocracy.  This is in sharp contrast to the lives of the 5000 tenants the first duke evicted during the Highland clearances.  The colossal statue of him nearby, is still a source of outrage to some, who want it removed.

Further down the coast we visited Dornoch, which claims to be **one of Scotland's sunniest spots**.  Dornoch was  the seat of the Bishops of Caithness in the 11$^{th}$ century,  and it has a well preserved cathedral, much of which was restored in 1924, returning it to its medieval appearance.  It has splendid stained glass windows, endowed by the Scots-American philanthropist Andrew Carnegie. Outside the cathedral is a dry fountain and the message appeared to be 'the spirit of God will sustain'.  We continued down, past the Glenmorangie Distillery, shame, and along the edge of the Cromarty Firth, which we then crossed to get onto Black Isle, which is neither black or an island but a peninsular in the Moray Firth.

We found Fortrose Bay site with no difficulty and parked on the edge of the beach with stunning views across the firth.  This was one of Alan's favourite pitches, as it felt 'almost private'.  We were told that we may see dolphins, so we watched attentively as we prepared and ate our breaded fish, but we didn't see any.

127 miles   **Total = 3725**

## SATURDAY 18TH MAY, 2019

It rained in the night and drizzled as we got up and went into Fortrose for gas and other provisions at the busy Co-op. Our first damp day of that section of the TRB.

We drove off the Black Isle and, again, past Inverness. This is a shame as, although the garage that repaired our motorhome was excellent, there is a lot more to this 'capital of the Highlands'. It was granted city status in 2000 and maintains a strategic position significant in Scotland's history. It changed hands between Scots kings, local clan chieftains and English invaders until the final defeat of the Jacobites at nearby Culloden in 1746, after which there was some stability in the Highlands. Crazily, we also pressed on past Culloden, scene of the **final battle fought on Scottish soil**, where Bonnie Prince Charlie made his last stand before abandoning his loyal followers and fleeing back to France. This event marked the end of Stuart ambitions to reclaim the British throne from the Hanoverians. More than 1,500 Jacobites and 50 Hanoverians died in less than an hour in this bleak place. As I write, the significance of my mother's middle name, Stuart, has just occurred to me. I do recall that the family were not impressed by the 'Campbells' and may well have been perplexed to have her marry an Englishman, even though his surname was Bruce.

We drove up the side of the Moray Firth to Fort George, built in response to the Jacobite uprising of 1745. It is the **finest example of Georgian military architecture in Britain** and still serves as a military garrison. We continued on past Nairn and went round Forres several times before eventually finding the impressive Sueno's Stone. This thousand year old Pictish cross-slab is situated in a suburban setting, behind a roundabout and is well protected by a huge glass box. Made of sandstone, it is intricately carved in five sections with vivid scenes of an unidentified bloody battle. It may record a Dark Ages victory by the Scots over a tribe of the northern Picts. Others believe it is named after an 11th century Danish monarch, Sweyn Forkbeard, the **first Dane to become ruler of England** and father of the more famous Canute.

We drove along the side of Findhorn Bay to the village of Findhorn, but saw no evidence of the new age settlement there. Along the coast to Lossiemouth, which had an airbase and much evidence of the fishing industry. For most of the rest of the day fishing was very much to be seen with sturdy stone harbours appearing at regular intervals. However, we did have to go inland to Elgin and then back to Buckie, where a much older Scottish cousin used to live. He worked in forestry and, indeed, the whole area was heavily forested. Robbie no longer lives there, but it would have been nice to visit him. Buckie itself appeared rather dull but other villages we passed through were well kept and painted. It is perhaps unfortunate that we got to Cullen midmorning and not the time to be eating Cullen Skunk, much as I love it. There is a large hotel at Cullen which claims to make award winning Cullen Skunk, sounded delicious.

We stopped for coffee at Portsay, which has a large and pretty seventeenth century harbour. Dolphins are often seen along this stretch of coast, but not when we were there. However, on a mound above the harbour there is a large wire model of a dolphin. In the harbour below Eider ducks were bobbing around, quite merrily. The weather became quite foggy as we passed Banff, and continued to our next campsite at Macduff. It was ok, and we were greeted by several children who were very eager to help us! Alan gave them some rubbish to take to the bins and they seemed quite happy with that and a biscuit each. Alan cooked Pork in

Cider from the Co-op, but we were distracted / entertained by a car that arrived beside us. From this car emerged the driver and his wife, then two dogs were freed from the back just as, one by one, four stiff teenagers fell from the back seats. Having visited the toilet block they all set to work, extracting and erecting a very large tent, bedding and cooking equipment, all in a very short time. We were impressed and even more so when they packed up and were ready to leave, before us, in the morning.

122 miles **Total = 3847**

## SUNDAY 19TH MAY, 2019

The weather was slightly clearer as we set off on high cliffs with views of the North Sea. We didn't manage to see the lighthouse museum at Fraserburgh but loved the miles of sandy beaches. Fraserburgh is **the largest shellfish port in Scotland** and one of the largest in Europe. Kinnaird Lighthouse was the **first lighthouse on mainland Scotland**, built in 1787.

We enjoyed our coffee watching gulls on the rocks in a sandy bay before setting off again by taking a 90 degree turn south on the A90. Peterhead is **Scotland's most easterly town** and it has an attractive stone port. In the 19th century Peterhead was a leading whaling port, turning later to herring and later to white fish. It was once Europe's premier white-fish port, but over fishing and the European Union's quotas have made the future uncertain for this town. It now serves as a supply base for northsea oil and gas rigs. We then drove south to Aberdeen where my mother went to secondary school and where my Godfather and his family lived when I was younger. My cousin Dorothy has now moved to London. We drove along a long attractive promenade to Old Aberdeen and the port area. During the Middle Ages, Aberdeen was one of Scotland's most important seaports trading wool, salted cod and haddock to Europe and importing timber, textiles and tools. Until the second half of the 20$^{th}$ century, Aberdeen was home to Scotland's biggest fishing fleet but as that declined, the discovery of huge reserves of oil beneath the North Sea, in the late 1970's, changed the city dramatically.

As we sat in an excellent parking position overlooking the River Dee, we watched large vessels going in and out of the port, one of which was guided by tugs and appeared to be carrying enormous stacks, probably for an oil rig. We walked to the large Marine Control centre, where we believe a friend, who now lives in Westleton, used to work. David and Elaine were pleased to leave Aberdeen and return to the warmer south. The sun was continuing to shine as we drove down to beautiful Stonehaven, however it was very busy and we couldn't find a parking space, so we drove through slowly and, then, continued on to Dunnottar Castle, one of **Scotland's most spectacular ruins**. This intriguing castle, which once held Scotland's crown jewels, was originally built in the 12$^{th}$ century but little remains of buildings from that time. Further buildings were added in the 14$^{th}$ and 16$^{th}$ centuries and these are joined to the land by a narrow, crumbling neck of rock with great cliffs on the sides.

We walked down towards the castle but it was too vertiginous for me to cross over to the castle itself. Strangely, I can't remember being brought here on any of our many holidays to visit my mother's family, when I was a child. Next, with use of the satnav, we found our way to Chapel of Barras, where my grandparents retired to, probably around 1930, when my mother was still at school in Aberdeen. It was very isolated and it must have taken her ages to get to school. The little cottage, attached to a farm, to which my aged grandfather was an advisor, is now a Bed and Breakfast, which both Norma and Alison have previously visited. We allowed ourselves a night in the B&B and found the couple running it (David and Michelle Drinkwater) to be very charming and welcoming.

We were shown round the cottage and told about the original buildings and just before we went in to the kitchen, Michelle told us that they had removed many years of coverings to get back to the original stone fireplace with built in salt alcoves and, as we entered there it was, as 100 years ago, together with a smiling apparition of my grandmother. Wow, weird, a vivid imagination??? It was quite affecting, but pleasant and warmingly reassuring. My grandmother died one month after I was born, so she knew of me, but we never met and my mother was unable to go so far north from Kent in 1949, with a month old baby, to her mother's funeral. How sad.

In the evening, the Drinkwaters dropped us off at a fantastic fish restaurant in Catterline, where we had a lovely meal before getting a taxi back.

(For mileage see next day.)

## MONDAY 20ᵀᴴ MAY, 2019

We didn't sleep too well but had a superb Full Scottish breakfast. Alan said it was his best ever! Michelle gave us one of her freshly baked wholemeal loaves and we headed off to Inverbervie, where my Godmother lived when I was a child. This was our base, every few years, when we went to visit my mother's family in Scotland, initially in my father's Austin 7. It is not the prettiest of towns but I have such an affection for it, as I did for my auntie So So (long story). Alan and I walked on the shingle beach but it wasn't as noisy as I remember it being when high seas grasped at the pebbles, such an evocative sound. We then drove on to Gourdon where my grandparents and aunt are buried. Sadly, I hadn't thought to take flowers with me to put on their graves. Gourdon is an ancient fishing village with a pretty natural harbour and a strong maritime heritage. Around the harbour wall there are posters giving information about the history of the village and its natural history. At the little fresh fish shop and smokery on the harbour, we bought some hot smoked salmon to have for lunch with the freshly baked bread we had been given in the morning.

After all this emotional family stuff, we drove on south, via Montrose and Arbroath to Dundee, where we parked near the 'Discovery' Point. We went into the restaurant for tea, but were ignored by the assistant, possibly after she discovered that we were English? We left.

Dundee has one of the most spectacular settings of any Scottish city, with the Sidlaw Hills behind, the Fife shore to the south and the North Sea to the east. Dundee was an important port in medieval times and has managed to diversify with changing fortunes, having been a flax-weaving centre, cotton weaving centre and later jute. In 1797, James Keiller opened the **first ever**

**commercial marmalade factory** here, an enterprise that grew to export its products all over the world. The Royal Research Ship 'Discovery', which made its first journey to the Antarctic under the command of Captain Scott, is now Dundee's top attraction. It is a very impressive vessel with triple masts and a single funnel and was designed to be powered by both sail and steam. We took good photos from outside but didn't go in as we didn't have time to justify the cost. We then set off, over the Tay Bridge and onto St Andrews and the East Neuk peninsular, Fife. We found our inland site, which was large and fairly empty.

Mileage for the two days  202  **Total = 4049**


## TUESDAY 21ST MAY, 2019

We woke at 6am, showered, filled motorhome and set off early to visit St. Andrews. Being early, we found parking on the main street and we walked to see the ruined cathedral, founded in 1160, which was once the largest in Scotland. Along the bay we passed the smart University buildings. St. Andrew's University is the **oldest in Scotland** and the third oldest in Britain. We walked further along the bay to visit the remains of the castle, rebuilt around 1390. Further along, stands the Royal and Ancient Golf Club, founded in 1754. With six courses, this is **Europe's largest golfing complex** and home of the British Golf Museum. Some version of the game is thought to have been played on the dunes at St. Andrews as early as the 12th century.

After returning to the motorhome we drove along the coast to Crail, one of five celebrated villages of East Neuk, meaning corner. Crail is the most easterly of the villages and has a charter going back to 1178. It is a very pretty village and has an attractive 16th century harbour, where we could hear puffins but not see them. We drove through the other villages and stayed on the coast to Kirkcaldy, where we ate our hot smoked salmon bought the previous day. Delicious. We both then had a little sleep, I think that two weeks of driving and concentrating was making us quite weary. After our rest, we drove down the side of the Firth of Forth, over Kincardine Bridge with views of the mile long Forth Rail Bridge, a triumphant celebration of 19th century's faith in industry and science. This bridge was the **world's first great steel structure** and it was declared a UNESCO World Heritage Site in 2015. From there, it wasn't far to our site near the sea on the outskirts of Edinburgh.

72 miles **Total = 4121**


## WEDNESDAY 22ND MAY, 2019

No driving today, we took the bus to visit Edinburgh, one of Britain's most spectacular cities. I visited here fairly often as a child, staying with my uncle, aunt and cousins Peter and Marilyn, but Alan had not been to Edinburgh before. Today, our first stop was the Royal Yacht Britannia, sitting in Leith's rejuvenated waterfront. The 125m long ship cost more than £2 million to build and was used for royal tours, private holidays and honeymoons away from the world's press. It was a fascinating visit and audio tour and very good coffee was served in the restaurant. Surprisingly, the Queen's rooms were quite modest and plain. We then took another bus to the outside of the famous Edinburgh Castle, which has stood high on its volcanic cliffs for more than 900 years. There is evidence of a Bronze Age settlement on Castle Rock, as early as the ninth century BC. We walked up to the Esplanade, which was laid out in 1753 as a parade ground and now hosts the Edinburgh Tattoo. From here the large main gates lead to the rest of the castle. I believe I can recall an occasion when I was left behind inside the castle when the Scots Guards paraded through, my mother claimed she knew I was alright as she could hear me screaming above the sound of the bagpipes! We decided not to go in to the castle this time, so walked slowly down 'the Royal Mile' to see the Palace of Holyroodhouse, which is the Queen's official residence when in Scotland. Alan's legs were hurting, but he made it and we had a quick look at the new Scottish Parliament buildings before staggering onto a bus and back to the campsite.

## THURSDAY 23RD MAY, 2019

We left Edinburgh site at 9.45am and drove along the southern coast of the Firth of Forth and through Musselburgh. Musselburgh has extensive mussel beds along its shore and there is a beautiful large shiny, steel sculpture of a mussel on the sea front. The journey along this coast was quite slow, so we continued on through North Berwick, which has the remains of a Napoleonic era signal station on a high volcanic crop above the city. Four miles east sits Seacliff, which has **the smallest harbour in Britain**, with the entrance measuring just three metres.

We stopped briefly to admire Tantalon Castle and the splendid Bass Rock. Tantalon Castle is one of the most daunting in Scotland, perched on a high rock with sheer cliffs on three sides and a curtain of dusky sandstone to its front. From the 14th to the 16th centuries it was the stronghold of the 'Red Douglases', a family notorious for murder, plunder and treason. For miles along this coast Bass Rock can be seen, once the plug of a volcano and now an island inhabited by more than 150,000 gannets, whose droppings give the rock a white capped, almost snowy appearance. We progressed on into St Abb's Head, which was a beautiful little town with three pretty harbours and a poignant statue of a woman with a heavy herring basket on her back. St Abb's Head is surrounded by spectacular cliffs of red sand stone sculptured by wind and waves and housing thousands of sea birds, including fulmars, kittiwakes, guillemots, puffins and razorbills. A few miles further south and we crossed the border back into England, as always with a strange feeling of sadness on my part.

At Berwick-upon-Tweed we stopped for lunch at a pleasant garden centre and, then, were soon, back on the road. Before long, Holy Island could be seen, elegant as ever out in the distance. Shortly, after that Bamburgh Castle came into view, looking proudly over the coastline. We found our next site at Beadnell Bay, with no difficulty, and we went immediately into Seahouses, to plan our trip out to the Farne Islands.

99miles = **Total 4220**

# FRIDAY 24TH MAY, 2019

## NORTH EAST

We drove back to Seahouses from our site, and at 11.45am, got on our boat out to the Farne Islands. What a fabulous trip with sunny weather and loads of birds – gannets, guillemots, razorbills, plenty of puffins and an amazing number of nesting Arctic terns. The terns were nesting close to the paths we were taking and they were quite distressed by our presence, squawking and dive bombing as we progressed. Beautiful little birds and I was surprised that we were allowed to visit at this time of nesting. There were also Eider ducks, common terns and one Red Breasted Merganser. We spent a long time sitting and watching the puffins, which were busily popping in and out of their holes, always looking a mix of pretty and amusing. On our return, we drove to Beadneth, which has the **only west facing harbour on the east coast of England**. Nearby, is the the village of Craster, allegedly a village that inspired Turner.

The village smelt of the smokery, so that is where we went and bought smoked fish, probably as gifts for Carol, who we intended to visit on our way home, and Fiona, who likes fish and was watering our garden while we were away. As we drove along the coast we could see Dunstanburgh Castle, an imposing ruin, looking dramatic on the Northumberland coastline. This ethereal castle was the 14th century stronghold of John of Gaunt, who **was at one time**, **the most powerful man in England.** We stopped to view the castle but didn't visit, despite its being a National Trust property. The Northumberland coast is of the Carboniferous Age, **150 million years older than Jurassic** and formed 350 million years ago.

## SATURDAY 25TH MAY, 2019

For a long time we had looked forward to visiting Bamburgh castle and we arrived early to see this spectacular fortress. It is on a rocky outcrop where the Anglo-Saxon Kingdom of Northumbria was founded in 547 by King Ida. Its defences were added to over the years, yet it was the **first English castle to fall in the Wars of the Roses,** in 1464. We happily wandered round the castle inside and out, and were particularly impressed by the King's Hall, which was included as part of the rebuild in 1894, by Lord Armstrong. After a delicious, thick parsnip soup, we decided to revisit Holy Island, which we had spent much time at after our incomplete walk of St. Cuthbert's Way. (I later found that the pain in my feet was due to planter fasciitis.)

We enjoyed visiting Lindesfarne Priory again. It was here, in AD635, that St. Aiden of Iona founded a Christian settlement and the Lindesfarne Gospels were created here by the monks, renowned for their religious art. However, the monastery was destroyed by Viking raiders in 793. We didn't go out to the castle, now a holiday home, on this visit.

## SUNDAY 26TH MAY, 2019

We left in good time and followed the coastal road seeing lovely sandy beaches and, soon, a stunning castle by the road in Warkworth. We really didn't have time to stop as we were meeting Carol and family for lunch and then had to get home. But, seeing Warkworth inspired us for the next stretch of our RBT and we determined to restart that stretch at Warkworth.

We had a good journey down to Newark where we met up with Carol, Jacob and Stephanie, Alan's youngest grandchild, for lunch. Alan was really pleased to see them and it was good to get their news. After we left them, we journeyed home, very tired but having loved this long trip round the west, north and east of Scotland and the northeast of England.

Miles at Ashington 32  **Total = 4252**

# FINAL STRETCH OF OUR ROUND BRITAIN TRIP!?

## WEDNESDAY 2ND OCTOBER, 2019

On our way again, always such an exciting feeling. Two days before, we had left home and met Sarah, Lucy and Tom for supper, before staying at the Premier Inn, in Kettering. Then, the day before we went to Alison and Bob's for lunch, before visiting our dentist in Kettering and then driving to the Premier Inn at Mansfield where we met Carol and family for a meal at the Brewers Fare Inn.

We had a good breakfast and drove north in the sun to get to Warkworth Castle, just as we had decided four months previously. The ruins of Warkworth seem to rule the surrounding countryside and they were well worth the visit. The castle, started as a Norman motte and bailey, grew into a massive fortress, with a proud Great Tower, a great hall, great chamber, interconnected passages, kitchens and wine and food cellars. It still has a complete eight towered keep, added by the Percy family, who dominated the North during the later Middle Ages.

Having visited this great place we drove down the coast to our site at Whitley Bay, a delightful site on the edge of the sea with a view of the wonderful St. Mary's Lighthouse, opened in 1898. As the sun began to go down, the lighthouse appeared increasingly pink, occasioning many photos. We were so enthralled, that when we realised that Alan had accidently brought homemade chicken stock instead of homemade chicken casserole, we were not too fazed, but neither of us can remember what we ate instead.

10 miles of new coast   **Total = 4262**

## THURSDAY 3ʳᴰ OCTOBER, 2019

We set off just before 9.30am and soon arrived at Tynemouth Priory and Castle, just on opening time. It was cold but clear and there were stunning views of the coast from the high, rocky headland on which the castle stands. It commands the entrance to the River Tyne and is known as the gateway to Newcastle. There was originally an Anglo-Saxon monastery here but this was destroyed by Vikings, and later a medieval monastery was founded here. It was later fortified against the Scots and became **one of the largest defended areas in England.** The site was large and interesting, but most striking were the stained glass windows in the chapel, particularly a round window facing east. Overlooking the Tyne is a vast statue of Collingwood, Nelson's second in command. This fortress headland continued to guard the entrance to the Tyne until 1956.

We drove along the north side of the Tyne, under the tunnel and then back along the south side of the Tyne, through South Shields to Marsden Bay. When we walked Hadrian's Wall, a few years ago, we started at Wallsend and went west along the Tyne for many miles.

Marsden Bay is home to one of the most important seabird colonies in England, with kittiwakes, fulmars, gulls and cormorants living on the stunning Permian Magnesium Limestone rocks which rise from the sea. These rocks were formed nearly 250 million years ago and continue to be of **interest to geologists worldwide.** We decided not to take the lift or the stairs to the beach below but did read some of the stories of smugglers who roamed the shores in earlier days.

After having coffee in the motorhome, we drove on to the red and white stripped Souter Lighthouse, which sits in a quiet place looking out over the North Sea. Souter was the **first lighthouse in the world designed and built to be lit by electricity**. Alan climbed the 76 steps to the top of the lighthouse, while I wandered outside admiring the beautiful sea and sky. At the top, Alan had been interested by the way the lighthouse lamp floated in mercury creating almost frictionless bearings. The guide was asked whether this open container of mercury was a health hazard, but the guide hadn't been able to answer this. Alan was mindful of the precautions that he had needed to take in his surgery, regarding mercury. Before we left we had delicious bowls of lentil and vegetable soup in the NT café and bought some environmentally friendly products in the NT shop. Their 'mint multi surface cleaner' smells gorgeous and is to be recommended. Driving further south we arrived at Hartlepool and visited the National Museum of Royal Navy Life and the Historic Quay.

Alan was very uncertain about going into the museum as we still had a long journey ahead of us. However, we did go in and were very pleased that we did. As you enter the quay the HMS Trincomalee majestically welcomes you, with mighty masts and cannons poised. The Trincomalee is **Europe's oldest floating warship** and is a jewel in the heart of the historic quayside. It was originally built in 1817 and when you climb on board and stoop to go round the quarters and stores, you get some idea of how difficult life must have been on board. Outside and all around the quay are recreated the shops, printers, tailors and instrument makers selling everything from guns, swords and an array of other desirables. Fortunately it wasn't busy when we visited and so we could appreciate the museum at its best. Following this visit we were behind schedule and this wasn't helped by finding the Tees Transporter Bridge closed. This is **the longest working**

**transporter bridge in the world** and I would have enjoyed crossing on it.

However, it was closed for repairs and traffic soon built up as the mass of workers streamed out of the large industrial units. Needless to say, we didn't get to the centre of Middlesbrough, the town where **Britain's greatest seaman and explorer, Captain Cook,** was born. Because of the 'snarl up' and the engine warning flashing again, we missed Redcar and cut across the corner to hasten our journey down to our site near Whitby, on the North Yorkshire and Cleveland Heritage Coast, where we arrived at 6pm. Alan's first job was to top up the coolant, which had fallen below minimum. Fortunately, this extinguished the warning light.

99miles **Total = 4361**

## FRIDAY 4TH OCTOBER, 2019

We left the motorhome on the site and took buses to visit the locality, mainly in the rain. First, we went to Robin's Hood Bay, where we last visited in 1998 having walked Wainwright's Coast to Coast Walk for our honeymoon. Although I made it there, it was with paracetamol to reduce my fever, which we later found was caused by pneumonia. Happy memories. On this occasion, we walked slowly down the steep road from the bus to the harbour and wandered through this pretty village, previously renowned for its fishing and smuggling. The wide bay is a geologist's wonderland. As the tide drops, broad rock platforms stretching 550m out to sea are exposed. This great reef is ribbed with hard, fossil filled limestone strata. Unfortunately the tide was in, so again, we were not able to walk out to them. We enjoyed visiting the Old Coastguard Station, which is now a visitor centre with interesting displays of the area's geology and sealife.

Next we took the bus back to Whitby, where we walked through the town and had lunch by the river, not at the famous Magpie, where I had fish and chips with some Wellingborough ramblers, when I walked the Coast to Coast with them in 1994. This town was Alan's mother's favourite place and we have a painting of hers which was painted for her by a colleague at the school where she taught. Whitby was a busy herring port for a thousand years before the whaling boom of the 18$^{th}$ century transformed the town. Melville's 'Moby Dick' makes much of Whitby. James Cook began his seafaring career here in 1746 and all four of his ships of discovery – the *Endeavour, Resolution, Adventure and Discovery* – were built in Whitby. We decided to visit the 7$^{th}$ century cliff top abbey the next day and, instead, returned to the buses and went to visit Runswick Bay, where a couple of weeks later Alison and Bob would be staying along with Becka, one of their daughters, and her family.

We walked slowly down the very steep road into the pretty village and admired the sweeping bay, which was beautiful, despite being covered in mist. After having a cup of tea in a little café above the beach, Alan noticed a stag proudly standing high on the headland, too far away to photograph but still impressive. The walk back up the hill to the bus was taxing for Alan, but we were warmed by the thought of another meal at the pub near our campsite.

## SATURDAY 5TH OCTOBER, 2019

### EAST

We left the site before 9.30 and went to Sainsbury's for a sizeable shop, including stretchy black trousers for me and a rugby shirt for Alan. We then went to Whitby Abbey in its splendid clifftop setting, towering over the town and the sea. The Benedictines founded this abbey in the 11$^{th}$ century after 9th century Vikings destroyed the original church established by St. Hilda in 657. In 664, the Synod of Whitby was hosted here, a significant event in the development of English Christianity, at which the **determining of the date of Easter was established**. The stark, brooding ruins inspired Bram Stoker to make Whitby the landing place for his fiendish vampire in 'Dracula'.

Back in the motorhome, we travelled on to Scarborough, **the oldest resort in the country**, which started receiving visitors in the 17$^{th}$ century, due to the discovery of mineral springs. There are two sandy bays divided by a proud headland on which Scarborough Castle sits. Bronze and Iron Age relics have been found there, together with Roman remains and evidence of Saxon and Norman chapels. There are also the remains of a Viking camp, said to be built by Scardi (or 'harelip'), after whom the town is said to be named. We found the south Bay, overlooked by the massive Grand Hotel, to be very touristy. North Bay was much more attractive and there were crowds of surfers enjoying the waves. All along the seafront were hundreds of VW Camper vans, presumably out for an arranged rally. Nicola would have loved it. Further south was Filey with a magnificent long sandy beach.

We didn't take the narrow road to Bempton cliffs, which has the **only mainland gannetry in England**. It also has the second largest puffin colony in the country. The **largest is on St.Kilda**, which we very fortunately managed to visit whist on a sea expedition to the Outer Hebrides, in 2013.

Continuing on, we went out to North Landing, also known as Flamborough Beach, where we ate our smoked salmon sandwiches before walking to admire the beach, stunning chalk cliffs and interesting caves. There were wonderful views of Selwicks Bay and the North Sea.

Driving inland and out again we went to Flamborough Head, with 400 foot high cliffs topped by two standing lighthouse towers, the oldest dating from 1669, and Flamborough Head Lighthouse built in 1806. We drove through Bridlington, the southernmost resort on the Yorkshire coast. It also has a stunning sandy beach and a harbour which is almost a thousand years old.

The road down to Withernsea was long, winding and away from the coast so rather tedious. We were surprised to find a white, inland lighthouse at Withernsea, about which, apart from it now being a museum, we have been unable to find much information. We found our next, certificated, site not far away at Hollym. There was one other motorhome on the site and we were placed just beside the toilet block. This turned out to be a good thing as it rained, but inside the newly refurbished interior there was no heating and only cold water in the taps. Clearly, there would be no showering the next morning. However, we settled in to our warm little home to make soup with the stock that we hadn't intended to bring, and accompanied that with a glass of wine, cheese and 'Strictly'! Lovely.

96 miles **Total = 4358**

## SUNDAY 6ᵀᴴ OCTOBER, 2019

It rained and the wind blew all night. We had boiled eggs for breakfast and set off, after paying, at 9.50am. The site owner explained his plans and apologised for the lack of warm water, but didn't offer a reduction. It was still raining and misty when we got to Spurn Heritage Centre. It is an interesting centre with helpful staff, but they could do nothing about the weather and our inability to see the renowned black and white lighthouse. It is sad that we were unable to see any of the three mile spit of sand and shingle leading out to Spurn Head. Here is **the fastest eroding coastline in Europe** and it is expected that the remaining sea defences will be swept away in the next few years. After that the whole process of spit formation will, apparently, start again, a cycle lasting about 250 years. None of the thousands of migrating birds that stop off in this area were to be seen while we were there.

We continued back up this interesting peninsular, through Kinston upon Hull and over the Humber Bridge, at a cost of £1.50! This masterpiece of civil engineering, at 1410m, was the largest single span suspension bridge in the world when it opened in 1981. **It is still the longest in Britain** and remains **the longest single span suspension bridge in the world that can be crossed on foot or by bicycle.** There are an amazing number of fascinating statistics concerning this fantastic construction but I am intrigued by the fact that the towers are 36cm further apart at their tops than their bases, to compensate for the curvature of the Earth! Brilliant.

Once into Lincolnshire, we headed for Immingham, which appeared very industrial and then through Grimsby, which had a large harbour and went on to Cleethorpes, which has a massive sandy beach. We stopped on the seafront to admire the beach, in the rain, and eat our sandwiches, but as our parking ticket fell irretrievably under the dashboard, we decided to move on rather than buy another ticket. Further round the coast we stopped at Saltfleet National Wildlife Park, where we took advantage of the sun and had a lovely walk out towards the sea. However, it soon began to rain again and we didn't see any wildlife, although we did see loads of sea buckthorn berries on the sea buckthorn bushes. These berries are edible and nutritious but we didn't try them. At Mablethorpe we were very close to the sea but the view was completely obscured by the amusements. Soon after that we went to our site at Sutton on Sea, a very pleasant place with lots of trees.

104 miles **Total = 4462**

## MONDAY 7TH OCTOBER, 2019

We set off in good time at 9.30ish and headed towards Skegness. This 'traditional seaside town' is renowned for its beaches but, again, we were unable to see them due to the density of amusement arcades. We should have continued on the same road through the town but something went wrong. Despite suggesting that we were going west instead of south, I was urged on! About an hour later we were back on the A52 and driving down the side of the Wash, but being The Wash, we were a long way from the sea. We drove through Boston, which had numerous rivers/tidal inlets. Boston was England's second largest seaport for much of the medieval period, when there was a flourishing wool trade with Flanders. It was at that time that local merchants built the magnificent St. Botolph's church.

The tower of this church was built without a spire, earning it the nickname the 'Boston Stump'. It was still the highest church tower in England. Another regret, we didn't stop to visit this remarkable church.

Fortunately, we did visit RSPB Frampton Marshes, where we had a delightful walk over the salt marshes and where we saw, and were able to identify, many birds. Greenshanks, Brent Geese, Greylags, Plovers, Egrets, Widgeon and Teals. There was undoubtedly, a whole lot more.

Continuing round the flat, salt marshy coast we missed the turning for King's Lynn, so didn't visit the historic town that was once part of the Hanseatic League, the commercial powerhouse of medieval Europe. We didn't feel that we needed to visit the impressive Norman keep of Castle Rising Castle again having cycled to it previously, when we were staying at Sandringham campsite. It was only when we got to Hunstanton that we saw the sea again. Big generous expanses of the North Sea, seen from many directions. It is here that The Wash ends and the Norfolk coast begins.

Always lovely, we have visited the Norfolk coast many times. As we drove through pretty Thornham we recalled staying at the Chequers Hotel for a few days when Alan was gaining strength and confidence following his heart surgery. We drove through the attractive Wells-Next-The-Sea, which in Tudor times was one of the great ports of eastern England, and then on to Blakeney and had a nostalgic walk along the harbour wall. Blakeney, was a village we went to often when Nicola was little, as friends, Judy and Peter invited us to join them there and then allowed us to go on our own. Later, Judy let Alan and I go there, so we have many happy memories of the town and the surrounding area.

We then drove on to the final site of our RBT, just before Cromer. The site was high on a cliff with spectacular views over the coast and the sea. We had a pleasant supper in the site restaurant.

154 miles   **Total = 4616**

## TUESDAY 8TH OCTOBER, 2019

We woke early to a clear sunny day and outside the air smelt beautifully fresh, and the view over Cromer Bay was delightful. Alan got chatting to a man on the site, and so we left at our usual time of 9.30am. We filled up with diesel and bought sandwiches near the pier enabling me to take a quick photo of the pier before setting off. We took the minor road along the coast, viewing the sea from time to time. At Bacton, the massive Gas Terminal loomed over the sea and countryside. It is a complex of six gas terminals and is a hydrocarbon Gas processing plant of strategic importance, making it understandable why that part of the coast is to be reinforced.

We drove on and saw the red and white stripped Happisburgh lighthouse, **the oldest working light in East Anglia** and the **only independently run lighthouse in Great Britain**, having been saved by the local community. It is maintained and operated entirely by voluntary contributions. We stopped at Sea Palling to admire the award winning beach and enjoy our coffee. Soon after driving on, we came to Waxham and were stunned by a beautiful Elizabethan barn about which we had no previous idea. On exploration we found that this Great Barn, built in 1570, is 178 feet long and is **one of the largest barns of its age in the**

**country**. It had only recently been restored and was awesome to stand inside. It is now open to the public with interesting visual displays of its history and also has a shop, café and can be used as a wedding venue.

Our next stop was at the Horsey Windpump, where we took a photo, observed the boats enjoying the Broads and recalled having had a long walk in the area, which had included blackberrying. The present windpump was built in 1912 on the foundations of the 18$^{th}$ century Horsey Black Mill. It was working until it was struck by lightning in 1943, after which it was acquired by the National Trust. Now fully restored, it is complete with winding cap and sails. Following that we stopped briefly at Winterton on Sea, where we had walked several times. Unfortunately we were unable to park the motorhome, a sadly common occurrence, so continued on.

Continuing towards our final destination, we drove through busy Great Yarmouth, a town with an interesting history but now best known as a hectic tourist resort. In the 10$^{th}$ century it was a fishing hamlet and it grew with the fishing industry, later supplying ships sailing off to major battles. Nelson embarked and returned here many times, notably after the Battle of the Nile in 1798.

In later years, from the 1960's, North Sea oil brought an oil-rig supply industry that now services offshore natural gas rigs. Off shore wind power and other renewable energy sources have led to further support for the town. The Time and Tide Museum is set **in one of the UK's best preserved Victorian herring curing works** and is **Norfolk's third largest museum**. It is said that some of the gunpowder plotters met here and when we visited with Ruth, a few years ago, Alan and his sister dressed up in plotters clothing! I didn't join in. Great Yarmouth was described by Charles Dickens' character Peggotty in 'David Copperfield' as the 'finest place in the universe'.

We drove on to Gorleston and had lunch on the promenade with distant views of Lowestoft Ness. We then followed the coastal road as closely as possible in order to get to the Ness. Great! We had done it! It was sunny and it felt very satisfying. We asked a very pleasant couple who were there, to take photos of us at our completion point. It emerged that they belonged to Geo-Suffolk and had designed the plate on the 'Geology of Westleton Common', which had recently been erected on the common - small world.

58 miles **Total = 4674**

Such an exciting adventure and achievement.

Nearly 5000 miles in 63 days.

Writing up this journal has been enormous fun both for Alan and me, and it has brought back many happy memories.

Before starting the tour, I had used many sources to inform us of places of interest that would be worth visiting. These included television programmes, walking magazines, AA Guides to Cornwall, Scotland and Wales and the very special Readers Digest book 'The Most Amazing Places to Visit in Britain'. This excellent book was a gift, but, unfortunately, we can't remember from whom.

During the course of writing, much of it in 'Lockdown', I used leaflets and guides acquired 'enroute', plus National Trust and English Heritage Handbooks. Also, of course, the internet has been extremely informative.